HARPER ADAMS

DARK PSYCHOLOGY SECRETS

Unmasking Covert Manipulation, Persuasion, and Psychological Warfare (2024 Guide for Beginners)

Contents

Chapter 1 : Introduction to Dark Psychology

If you are not aware of the dark side of psychology, then you might very well be under the control of others. No matter what you might have experienced while under the power of those around you, where it all starts is within our own head. The brain is a complex organ that is capable of an incredible amount of various skills. Some of us look alike, and some of us even think alike, but very few people will have brains that match each other. Even identical twins will have their own individual personalities. Out of all the organs within our body, the brain might just be the one that we're never going to be able to fully understand. It is one organ that we can't replace through transplants from other people, and we will not be able to improve our brains or use artificial parts when ours aren't functioning properly. Because of all this, it is easy to start to understand just how complex thinking patterns can become.

We can understand the reasons that we do the things we do. There's always an argument about whether nature defines who we are, or if it is the nurture that we receive growing up that really helps to decide the way that we think. Most would agree now as opposed to in the past that it is a combination of both. The genetic makeup you were born with combined with the things that you experienced as you were raised will help to decide what it is about your brain that leads you to think and act in the way that you do. For this reason, we are able to start to understand what factors might drive our impulses and the patterns of thought that lead us to the decisions that we make.

Dark psychology starts to make us question what might be lying deeper underneath just the initial surface of the human mind. It is easy to see that you go to the fridge to get a snack because you are hungry. You find a partner you love because you want to have someone to go through life with. You get a job so you can have money to buy the things you want and need. But what about everything else? What causes a person to want to control someone else? To manipulate them? To emotionally harm them? This is the part of psychology that we will be discussing throughout this book. It is not about the natural animalistic impulses that help lead our path through life. It is the darker part of our worlds that lead us to act deviously that we really want to understand throughout this book. Our brains are complex organs that create the center of who we are. You pick up things from other people as you grow in this world. You are taught directly and indirectly how to act. You're told that you should be kind to other people and that you should treat your loved ones with respect.

However, there might be instances, such as witnessing marital abuse, that might teach you that violence is the way to act on your emotions. Although you might be taught to say, "please and thank you," in school, you might also have had rude parental figures who took advantage of others, teaching you how to be rude yourself. Though not many people will teach their children to directly be mean, emotionally manipulative, or controlling, it is certainly something that could still easily happen.

There are billions of neurons in your brain, all of which have the power to store information. Whenever you learn new information, new connections are created within your brain. We have an endless amount of storage in our brain—or seemingly endless, at least—so we are truly capable of learning anything. Not everyone is aware of this great power, and rather than nurturing a growth mindset, many people will just stick to the things that they already know. They can fall into unhealthy patterns that lead to unhealthy decisions, and eventually, they might lose the ability to have control over their own lives because they will not always know how to pull themselves out of the rut they've fallen into.

We all make our own decisions, but it is easy to feel as though you don't have that power based on the things that you might have experienced. Your brain is a complex organ that isn't just made up of one big part. Instead, it is multiple parts that work harmoniously together in order to help you survive in this world as best as possible. Signals are sent throughout your brain that let other parts know what needs focus and attention at the time. You start to unknowingly train your brain as you navigate through this world.

Eventually, you become accustomed to reacting to certain things in different ways, and so your brain will get used to responding as you have in the past. This is seen in how some people might lash out at the first sign of stress, or they might naturally respond to anger with violence without even thinking about it. Even though someone might be stuck in their ways, they can still get out of this pattern with a little mental effort. Our intelligence levels are based on many different factors. We have intelligence that we gain from reading books, watching movies, and doing other academic things. We then have our ability to be logical and reasonable, figuring out problems on our own without the help of outside sources. We also have our emotional intelligence that can assist in our ability to recognize our own emotions and the feelings and thoughts of others.

The better you can increase all of these types of intelligence, the better off you'll be in life. A big part of freeing yourself from dark psychology is to have a high level of emotional intelligence. The one true freedom we have in life is over our own minds and the ability to control our emotions. You can't control where you were born, the background you came from, your race, and many other things that you were given since the moment you entered this world. The one thing that you will always have control over—no matter what—is your ability to change the way that you think. No matter how stuck in a certain thought pattern you might feel, you will absolutely always have the ability to control your emotional reaction.

Other people can learn how to do this when we're not careful. If you are not in control of your emotions, then someone else might be able to take the reins. Those who are aware of how they can manipulate other people's feelings will target individuals with a low emotional intelligence level. Sometimes this is intentional, but other times we are just naturally drawn to certain types of people. It is time to take control of these emotions before someone else does.

Defining Dark Psychology

When interacting with others, you can either help them or hurt them. You can look at someone and think of a way to offer support, or you could look at them and see a way to use their emotional state as a way to gain an advantage over them. Brains are tools for surviving in this world, and like all tools, you can either use them to create something new or destroy something. If you were given a hammer, you could decide to create a new beautiful home using that hammer, or you could use it to destroy a house. The tool is just as it is. It doesn't change in either of those scenarios. What changes are the mindset, intention, and overall decision of what you are going to do with this tool. We're taught to treat people kindly and help them to do better. It is a natural sort of unspoken rule that we should be loving and compassionate to your neighbors and look for ways to help others when we can.

The issue with this is that we aren't often taught why we need to do this. Instead, we're just given superficial sort of ideas as to how we should be nice to others. Say "please/thank you/I'm sorry/how are you? /have a nice day," and many more phrases that get tossed around frequently. These become basic memorized phrases that start to lose all meaning after a while. Throughout our lives, we're also taught how to hurt each other, even when it is not intentional. We're often told that everything is fine after hurting someone as long as you say "sorry." Because of this, we end up not fully believing everything that we're taught, and it becomes easy to forget

The Golden Rule as we age and navigate throughout our lives. Sometimes, if you are not actively trying to be a kind person, it can be easy to fall into a negative mindset with those feelings spreading to others. Sometimes, you're hurting so deeply that you might even be the abusers yourself. If you are harsh to yourself, always saying mean things and hurting yourself mentally, then it is rather easy to start to do this to others as well. Being a negative and abusive person can become the new normal because it might be the way that you have been treating yourself first.

At the same time, if you were abused as a child, then this is how you are taught to handle other people. This is the way that you believe the world operates, so it is easy to start to inflict that pain elsewhere. It is interesting to start to get to know the way that other people's brains work when using dark psychology. This is what dark psychology is all about. It is the how, why, and what of manipulation, control, emotional abuse, and all of the other challenging parts of how the brain works that dark psychology aims to unpack.

The negative treatment of other people is common in the world today. If you go to any big celebrity's Instagram account, you will see tons of hate comments on the picture. If someone has an issue with a worker at a restaurant, it is easy to go home and complain online, possibly getting that person in deep trouble with people in higher positions of power within the company. Even in your own personal and romantic relationships, it can sometimes feel more natural to just be hateful and mean rather than actively working to build your partner up and make them feel better overall. Now more than ever it is important that we start to really understand dark psychology in order to prevent these kinds of toxic patterns from spreading to others.

We all need to take charge of our own emotions and learn how to control them ourselves to create a happier and better world overall. Now we know what dark psychology is: It is the study of more challenging thinking patterns that we all might have. What are the motives and goals of those who wish to manipulate other people? This is an answer we will provide in chapter 2, but let's first look deeper at whether or not these darker thinking patterns exist within all of us.

Do We All Have a Dark Side?

The true question that haunts many is whether or not we might all have this dark side lying dormant within us. Even the kindest of people might have a deep and controlling manipulator within their own brains. Is it part of the human condition? It is still the animalistic part attached to us that we've had since primordial times? Were our dark minds passed down to us from our ancestors, or is it something forever wired in our biology?

erhaps we do all have a dark side. Whether or not this is true for everyone doesn't matter as much. The most important thing that we have to remember is that our mindset needs to be managed whether or not we really are happy or sad, positive or negative. Sometimes we start to think that we only need to nurture our emotions and keep them in check if they are negative. In reality, we should be conscious of the positive feelings that we have as well. It is crucial that we look deep within ourselves and analyze our lives in order to ensure that we are actually happy beings and not just faking it. If we suppress our emotions too often then this can be like shaking a soda bottle.

Eventually, it will pop. What is it to have a dark side? Ask yourself first what it means to have a darker mind. For those that state that they don't believe it is possible for them to have a darker side, we have to question if they just haven't looked deep enough at their own mental psyche yet. It can be scary to admit that you might have darker thoughts that you don't want to confront, but it is crucial that we are aware of these feelings so that we don't suppress them.

Think of those who are peaceful individuals. They might state they don't feel anger, but that isn't always healthy.

Anger can be dangerous, but it can also be good. It is not the feeling that matters, but the reaction to this feeling. Having a light or dark side doesn't mean being free from anger or under its control. Your dark side is the one that makes you want to punch someone who made you angry, and your light side might be the one that wants you to be kind to this person, maybe even helping them, after they have upset you. Those feelings exist within all of us, and we can decide whether or not to act on them based upon whether or not we are in tune with our "dark/light" side. What separates people from other animals is people's ability to empathize and to be intellectual. Your dog might come up to you and try to comfort you when you are sad, and this helps explain what sympathy means. To be empathetic means that you really understand what someone else is going through.

If you just lost your job, when you get home from work you might start wondering what you are going to do now that you've been let go, and you might start to cry. Your cat might come up to you and sit on your lap, or maybe your dog will even try to lick your tears. It will only be a friend, a partner, a family member, or another human that would really be able to empathize with you. They would be able to feel your pain and understand what you are going through and using intellectual abilities to give you advice, help to change your perspective or do something else that actually helps you rather than just makes you feel emotionally better at that moment. We still have these animal instincts that make us want to act impulsively.

Even though we are separated from other animals because of this ability to rationalize and think, we still can't pretend that we don't have these natural urges or thoughts that might lead us to destructive behavior. We all have a fight or flight instinct within us when we are threatened. You might ready your body, your muscles getting tense and your heart rate raising when you feel as though someone might potentially harm you. This is your body's natural way to help fight off or flee from anything that could really hurt you, both emotionally and physically. We've created societies that have helped to keep us civilized. The laws in place have helped us to control some of those animal instincts. That's not to say that everyone would be killing each other, but there would probably be a lot more people throwing punches and using weapons if that type of behavior didn't lead to legal trouble.

That is because it is easier to release tension when you are mad by throwing punches than by working through the psychological factors that play into why you might feel the need to physically or mentally harm someone else. What about the limits of the human mind? Who is the authority figure that is protecting us from being manipulated? These civilizations throughout time have helped to shape us into the functioning society that we are today. However, there are still legal limits that don't protect us from as much emotional abuse. Even acts like cyberbullying are hard to prosecute because we don't fully understand the intention or long-term effects of what this emotional abuse might do. There is no one policing thoughts entirely, so it can be much harder to break free from emotional control when someone else has manipulative skills.

Understanding Mind Manipulation

These ordered societies which prevent chaos also do something else for us. They provide us with other basic survival aspects we need. We have police officers, firefighters, and other types of public help that can assist us if we need it. We have hospitals and grocery stores that will provide us with the basic human survival necessities. Though we have plenty of outside sources to help keep this society running, there is still a lot more that we need to live a fully happy and healthy life. These are things that we will also need to find on our own, but not every person will be able to incorporate these aspects into their lives.

This includes things like finding a family and a network of support or finding a passion or a reason in life as well as having entertainment and art that help keep us fulfilled, extra money to spend on whatever we want, fashion to express ourselves, and all the other fun parts of life that extend beyond the bare minimum of what is needed for survival. Humans are a group species. This means that we need others to help us survive. Although some people might be able to survive all alone in this world if they have to, not everyone can say the same. Even if we don't physically need things from others, it is the emotional support that many of us are searching for in order to feel entirely fulfilled. What many don't realize is that we should be finding this emotional aspect all on our own. Our brains are self-preserving.

They are going to do whatever they have to in order to make sure that we are functioning properly and meeting all of our basic human needs. If our brains weren't trying to protect us, then many of us would have gotten into many more dangerous situations than we have experienced already. How do our brains help us? Well, for example, when you walk down the stairs, your brain helps you find each step to make sure that you don't just fall down all of them. If you go to eat something that smells rotten, your brain knows this is a signal that you shouldn't eat it or else you might get sick. Even those who have attempted suicide know that there is still that voice whispering not to go through with that plan. Pain causes us to take action and try to solve the problem.

Pain is what is used in order to keep you restricted and in this place of preserving yourself. If you touch a hot pan, your brain knows that you shouldn't pick it up. If you fell off your bike the first time you rode it, then your brain might tell you that you should stay away from bikes. A bite from a mean cat tells us not to be mean to cats anymore. What sometimes happens in our brains, however, is that we misinterpret this pain. We can become used to this pain, as well, and eventually become numb. This isn't a bad thing altogether. You can push past the pain of falling off the bike to get back on and keep practicing until you've mastered the ability to ride with no training wheels. You can push past the pain of running on a treadmill so that you are able to always increase your time and become healthier.

If we push past our mental pain too often, we become used to this and start to think that it is normal. Fear is also important in keeping us alive. Fear is what will tell you that the hill is too steep to ride down, that the dark alley is too scary to walk down at night, that the spider's nest in the corner isn't something that you should mess with. These fears can be heightened a lot depending on our minds, or we can calm ourselves down and work through these feelings.

Sometimes, we misinterpret these feelings. Fear can cause us to react emotionally in an unhealthy way. Both fear and pain can trigger stress, which is a reaction to our fight or flight instincts. We can start to look for cures in all the wrong places. This is why some people might become addicted to alcohol or drugs in order to numb the constant pain or fear. Not everyone can fully understand what this pain is and where it comes from. Because they are already such natural things in small amounts, as we gradually increase the fear or pain in our lives, this becomes normalized as well. We will not think that there is anything wrong with the way that we're living, so it becomes more challenging to try and break free from these emotional patterns. Since we are a group society, we might actually end up depending on other people in order to try and alleviate some of these feelings.

Manipulation becomes a survival tactic. Rather than looking deep within to overcome these feelings, it can be easier for some people to manipulate others in order to get what they feel like they need. You may start to control people so that they serve you and provide you with the basic survival needs that alleviate your fear and pain. When we aren't able to control our emotional states, then we look for control in any other way that we can in our lives. This is a mistake in our thinking patterns and how we interpret the need for desire and control. We think that having power over other people means that we have the power within our lives.

Our brains will think that having this status is what is going to help relieve us from the inner turmoil that we feel on a daily basis. This is when you can really start to understand mind manipulation. People aren't just natural sadists who manipulate you and others just out of sheer pleasure. Perhaps there are some people who do this, but a lot of manipulation is just a misguided attempt at taking back some of the power in their lives. What manipulators fail to realize is that no one else will ever be able to provide them with the happiness that they need to survive in this life. Mind manipulation is ubiquitous. We often think of it in terms of that overly angry, muscled, raging man who might be controlling his girlfriend. This is very common, but manipulation is also found within all genders, all shapes and sizes, and all different kinds of people.

Someone with very few muscles might be able to still control a group of people, so we should never equate manipulation with physical strength. It is a different kind of tool that is used by humans in order to serve their needs to alleviate fear and feel like they have power over other people. The media has been controlling your mind for a while now. Commercials, movies, TV shows, magazines, and books all have the ability to change the way that you think. The more you expose yourself to this kind of media, especially the same media over and over again, the easier it is to start to control you. There are basic manipulative tactics used, such as the bandwagon effect — "everybody's doing it." Then there are the more deeply embedded methods, such as commercials making their volume levels louder so that you can still hear the advertisement if you leave the room during a break in your show.

The point of this manipulation is to have control over the consumer in order to keep them buying the goods and services provided by the company being advertised. Those closest to you might be manipulators as well. It might be their personal way to try to alleviate the stress and emotional turmoil in their lives. It might also be a survival tactic because they depend on other people to provide them with the basic existence requirements that they need to have filled. Sometimes, we will not even realize that we might be trying to control others in smaller ways. Manipulation can be so deeply embedded that we are unaware that it is present in certain situations both on the giving and receiving end of either side.

The Benefits and Value of Persuading Others

It is not always a terrible thing to be able to mentally persuade someone. We have to start to understand the difference between manipulation and influence. Manipulation is full of evil intentions with self-serving goals that will take advantage of other people. Influence is when a common goal is desired that will help to make everyone's lives better, not just the person that is doing the influencing. Both might involve some similar tactics, but the intention is what should be different.

The issue here is that we need to ensure we are doing it for the benefit of everyone. Much of the manipulation that we're already experiencing is something that can keep us under control, whereas influence should be something that helps empower many. Think of it like this: Adolf Hitler was a manipulative individual who convinced others that they should follow orders to serve a dark purpose. He managed to convince an entire society that they should wipe out a massive group of people in order to fix an issue that was entirely unrelated to what ended up happening. Dr. Martin Luther King, Jr. was an influential leader who helped to empower first a small town and then an entire country. He helped others to see what they had been experiencing and managed to change the course of history, with positive effects that we can still see today. It is also important for you to be able to protect yourself. There is value in being an influential and persuasive person because it can lead you to get what you want.

Maybe you need a raise at your job, or you want to move to a new house with your spouse. If you can be a positive influence and understand how your words can bring you to a solution that is beneficial for both of you, it will help lead you to a happier and healthier life. It can keep the peace between you and a loved one. Disagreements can turn into ugly fights when both people are feeling defensive. If one of you understands how to be a positive influence, you can actually talk your feelings out, which may bring the two of you closer lead to a compromise that leaves both of you happy. When you can be persuasive, you will be able to better share your own emotions. It will be beneficial to understand both your own and the psychology of other people.

Throughout the remainder of the book, we are going to break down the specific ways that you have been manipulated. We are then going to show you all of the methods that can be used to help you better become that influential person yourself. The more open-minded you can be in this process, the easier it will be to understand the reality of some of your most challenging emotions. Your life, your personal world, and the world, in general, can be a much better place if we all start to learn the ways that we can positively influence those around us.

Chapter 2 : Understanding the Persuader and the Manipulator

There are signs that you can see to determine whether you are the manipulator or the one being manipulated. Sometimes when you are currently under someone's control, you may not be able to notice you are being manipulated, but as you go through your life and become more aware of your own feelings and the emotions of others, it becomes a lot easier to start to see the dynamics of your relationship. You might not be able to realize what is happening until much later in life after you've been entirely removed from the situation. This is why it is so crucial that we become aware of manipulation and the way that it affects us now more than ever. If we aren't careful, it becomes incredibly easy to fall under someone else's control.

It's important to understand that not all influence is necessarily a bad thing. There are plenty of people in the world that seriously need some guidance. Maybe they were already in an abusive relationship where they were the one who was the manipulator. It is not like those who are abusive are always doing so because it makes them happy. Positive influence can help people realize that what they are doing is wrong because they are often in situations where they think that what they are doing is the right thing.

Influence can also help those realize that they might be on the receiving end of this abuse. Women who have escaped from abusive relationships can help other women who are still trapped really understand the mind tactics used against them so that they can remove themselves in a healthy way. It can be hard to identify these kinds of manipulative people because they come in all different shapes and sizes. We often associate a scary physical appearance with being a scary person. This is incredibly far from the truth. Often, the biggest manipulators will hide behind a big smile and deceptive eyes.

They will not be wearing a badge that states that they are going to try and attempt to control us, so it is essential that we start to become more and more aware of the deeply embedded signals that help to let us know when someone might be a manipulator. These people will have all of the qualities of someone who does not want you to know their intentions. They have managed to disguise their manipulative methods behind a thick cloak they've created. If you break through this barrier, they will still have manipulative methods to try and cover their tracks.

A lot of manipulation is planned out, so they will be able to have backup plans if things don't go the way they envisioned. Manipulators love to have control, so they will be able to know how to orchestrate the situation in order to provide themselves with the biggest benefits in the end, leaving others to fend for themselves. Once you've fallen into a manipulator's grasp, it is hard to free yourself. They will usually have convinced you that you are crazy and that you are in the wrong. They will make you question your thoughts and doubt yourself so that your self-esteem is so low that you can't do anything but depend on this person. They might have isolated you, making it harder for your friends and family to make you aware of the deeply embedded web of control that you have fallen into. If you've known someone outside of a manipulative relationship, you understand how easy it is for you to see the lies, but for them, it is deeper than that.

The manipulator will often show their good side to the person that they are controlling, maybe making themselves seem emotionally vulnerable as well. They are good at revealing some of their kind personality in order to keep themselves looking human in the eyes of the person who should actually be seeing them as a monster. They will lie and trick you into believing something about themselves that isn't true, making it easier to instill guilt and fear into anyone that might question leaving the manipulator behind.

This might be because if we all have that dark side in us, those manipulators might have that good side in them. If you have found yourself on the receiving end of emotional abuse, then you know that part of you wants to help the other person. Hurt people can recognize emotional pain within others, and abusers certainly have a part of them that is deeply hurt. Rather than wanting to shut their abusers out of their lives, many victims will take on a certain responsibility for the emotional pain that abusers experience. Even though they know what the other person is doing is wrong, they can still make excuses.

They'll say things like, "he was abused too," or "he's had a really hard life." That might have been true, but all of us have experienced hurt, and that doesn't mean that it is OK to inflict that kind of pain onto other people. When you can take manipulation and use it for good, it transforms into influence. When you stop trying to take from other people and instead spread the positive knowledge that you might have acquired, this can create a healthy, long-lasting relationship. The more you are able to positively persuade people, the more of an influencer you can become.

Rather than just being someone who ignores emotions and just takes each feeling as it is, you can use all of these individual mindsets as ways to empower you and other people around you. Influencers aren't bad. They know how to inspire different perspectives in others. The greatest influencers in the world found something that needed to be changed for the greater good and decided to inspire others to do this. They wanted a better world for themselves, but they also realized that the best world would be one in which everyone was benefiting and thriving rather than just themselves.

Manipulators want to turn you into a puppet. They have their own individual needs that they will use you to try and fill. Influencers would rather have you be the puppeteer of your own world. They understand that people will be more useful for the greater good if they can think creatively and on their own. Manipulators understand that you will be able to serve their purpose better if they can control you, and they want to control you so that you do what's best for them and not just yourself. Manipulators want to exploit you while influencers would rather help you to thrive (Duncan, 2018).

Who These Individuals Are

Manipulators aren't always going to be aware that they are exhibiting unhealthy and potentially harmful behavior. Sometimes, they are simply lost in their delusions. Many abusers will have been through this themselves, so they will not think that what they are doing is necessarily wrong. Even when they might have moments where they question their behavior, their brains have become so adapted to their delusions that they will find a way to convince themselves that what they are doing is just and right. Manipulators will do anything they can to make sure that they are always cast in a good light. They will put other people down in order to make themselves look even better.

Rather than making fun of themselves, they will make sure others are the butt of the joke. The first sign that someone might be a manipulator is when they start to make jokes that only hurt other people in the process. These might be jabs at the way that someone looks, making everyone pay attention to their flaws so that those in the group are distracted from the manipulator's own shortcomings. They might joke about something that you said, making you feel dumb or stupid for sharing that phrase.

This can cause them to look even smarter because they brought the attention of something less-than-intelligent to the rest of the group. It is common for manipulators to make themselves the center of attention by creating a platform for making fun of others their personality traits. Sometimes, they will end up playing the victim. They might make you feel as though you hurt them by trying to bring up a way in which they actually hurt you. If you say to them, "I feel like you hurt me the other day," they can easily turn it back around on you by asking something like, "how could you think that of me? Don't you think I'm better than that?" They will distract you from the real issue, the biggest problem, all by turning it back around and making it all your fault.

Manipulators are really good at lying, so much so, that they have usually convinced themselves of their own lies. This is why even the evilest criminals will be able to fake their way through a lie detector test. They have convinced themselves so deeply to believe the lies that they've told that they will often have plenty of excuses to alleviate any accusations around their lies. They've already told these excuses to themselves in order to justify the lie in their brain, so it will be easier for them to recite the nontruths when they're confronted. They use their control in order to have power over you. They are highly aware of the way in which manipulation gives them the upper hand, and they are going to exploit this power as much as possible. It is important for them to have this high level of power because they will be worried that should the tables turn, you will hurt them just as much as they hurt you. If a manipulator is already given power without trying, they will exploit this like crazy as well

. Those who are in higher positions at work, those who have money, and those who have decision-making power will often use this to their advantage. Just look at individuals in the film industry who were exposed as recent victims of sexual abuse from prominent producers and other popular cast members who started to come forward about what they experienced. It was clear that they used their status and wealth in order to manipulate their victims and make them feel powerless so that they would give in to their demands. Then, even afterward, they were able to use their status in order to scare victims into silence, making these individuals feel as though they had no choice but to keep what happened to them a secret out of fear of retaliation.

They can belittle you and make you feel as though you are stupid. They'll use facial expressions such as scrunched eyebrows and dirty looks in order to keep you silent. They will mock you for the things that you say and ignore your thoughts all in an attempt to make you seem dumb. They will say things like, "what are you talking about," or, "you are not making any sense," in order to try and silence something substantial that you might actually be saying. Sure, what you share might not be the most intelligent thing at times, but no one should make you feel stupid for this. There are better ways of letting someone know that they aren't making total sense.

They often will try to make you seem as though you are crazy as well. If you bring something up to them, they might state something like, "you are remembering things wrong." They will outright lie in order to ensure that you think you are crazy. They will make you start to question your own memory, and therefore, start to question your own sanity. They will deny things as much as possible in order to better serve their delusions. They are going to make you feel crazy for bringing up issues, maybe telling you that you are overthinking it or that you are looking at something too deeply.

Manipulators will make you feel as though everything is your fault, and they will look for other ways to place blame. You will often hear many abuse victims state that an emotional or physical attack was their fault first for initially provoking the manipulator. Manipulators know that they still have to give a sense of control to their victims in order to keep them dependent, so they will give that control to the abused in the form of power over the abuser's emotions. They'll say things like, "you know that bothers me when you bring that up," or "you are making me really mad right now," when the victim tries to bring up times that the abuser might have hurt them. The abused will start to think that they are the ones with the problem and that they need to fix something about themselves; eventually, they will stop trying to help the abuser see their own negative patterns.

Manipulators can really drain your energy. They will completely suck the life out of you but provide nothing back to you. Your spirit will be stolen by these abusive individuals, and you will eventually have nothing left except for a shell of the person that you used to be. They will either keep you around forever as a loyal servant, or they will get tired and move onto the next victim. They will not care about the things that they did to you and will only live to serve their own intentions. Manipulators don't personally grow. Rather than looking within themselves and improving, they instead look to others and blame them from their unhappiness or dissatisfaction with life. Sometimes those you know might use some slight manipulation tactics. We all do from time to time without thinking of it.

What differentiates a manipulator from just a regular person with minor bad habits is that a manipulator will do whatever they have to in order to justify themselves. It is a pattern of abuse that you will see, whereas the average person will be able to look at themselves and grow within a toxic situation. What you will always be able to use to decide if it is manipulation or influence is an evaluation of the goal of the person who is trying to be persuasive.

The Goal of Manipulators Manipulators

will use you on part of their journey toward getting what they want. They have their own goals and desires, and rather than looking deep within themselves and controlling their own thoughts and emotions, they will start to control other people. Think about the last time you were on the couch relaxing and needed to get something from across the room. Maybe your phone was on the counter in the kitchen where your roommate was. It is easier to just ask them to get your phone for you and bring it to you rather than to get up out of your comfortable position and get it yourself, right? This is the kind of mentality that manipulators have. Of course, it is not manipulative to ask someone for a favor, but those who choose to manipulate others will know that it is easier to just have other people do things for them, so they will never bother to look deep within themselves and try to improve on their own.

Manipulators will feel as though they will not have control over their lives. Perhaps they haven't achieved a desired social status, or maybe they just don't have the patience to wait to obtain the things they want. They will look for methods of control by assuming power over innocent people. They will have gotten used to reacting on their emotions right away rather than thinking through them and working on them in a healthy manner, so this will lead to them looking for control more frequently than trying to work on themselves. They might feel alone and as if others are out to get them. They usually will have been isolated at one point, and they will likely have unhealthy relationships. This can make them feel alone.

Especially when you are in a power dynamic, it will be harder to connect with those beneath you if you maintain the restrictions of authority over them. This can be very lonely, so it is easy to start to feel as though everyone is against you. If you are a negative-thinking person, lack a feeling of control over a situation, and have isolated yourself from other people, then it is very easy to start to think of yourself with a "me vs. them" mentality. They could be dealing with their own immense pain and feel best when they can exert that over other people. Think of the last time that you became frustrated with a physical object. Maybe you were trying to fix something that was broken, or perhaps you dropped something on your foot. Though this object doesn't have any feelings, it can still feel really good to exert your power over this object and inflict pain back.

For example, think of someone who gets frustrated with their phone when it isn't working or grows angry while they're watching a sports game on TV. When things don't go their way, they might take it out on this object. This is because they feel as though they don't have power over the object that caused them the pain as it controlled their feelings. In an attempt to gain that power back, they hurt the object in order to stop themselves from feeling any more pain. They might feel as though their life isn't fair. They will fail to see the good aspects and instead only focus on the negative things in their lives. It will be very hard for someone who is manipulative to see the privileges that they have been granted, so they will end up feeling as though nothing is good in their life and that everyone is against them.

Even though manipulators seem to have power, they usually will be rather self-conscious. This will create a desire within them to improve their selfesteem. They will make themselves feel better only by putting others down. Rather than reflecting on themselves and admitting when they're wrong, they're going to be much more likely to point fingers at others who are "worse than them" in order to cause distraction from their own biggest insecurities. Sometimes they just simply hurt and are looking for a way to fill that pain by hurting others. It is a very lonely feeling to hold onto so much emotional pain, so they might be trying to desperately connect to someone else so that they don't have to go through the process of having so much emotional damage. Remember that just because they might have deep underlying reasons why they manipulate, this does not mean what they do to you is OK. We are all hurt in our own ways, and some of us choose to take that out on others, and some of us will not.

The Goal of Influencers

It is important to remember that not all manipulation has to be a bad thing. Again, whatever you discover behind the true intentions of whether someone is manipulating you or not is going to be their overall goal. Are they going to try to help you for the good of everyone or take advantage of you just for the benefit of one? Influence is when you know a great positive truth and want to share it with others. You might have discovered this on your own, or maybe you have been influenced by someone else and have decided to take that thought on yourself. Then you can spread that to others and create a better, healthier world where everyone is able to thrive rather than suffer.

If you manage to do this, then you are going to be able to positively help everyone around you. Books like this can be influential. As the author, it is import to convince those who are reading that they deserve to break out of the cycle of manipulation. As someone who has gone through this experience yourself, it is important to share messages with those who might be going through the same things in order to help them break from their fears. This could be a book about how to be manipulative yourself and the ways that you can use dark psychology to get what you want. Instead, we are going to focus only on spreading positive manipulation because that is what is going to be best for everyone in the long-run as well. Influencers will want to share their passion.

They will have discovered a greater truth and come to the conclusion that they know how to share it. Those who are influencers also have felt the pain that you have before. They have lived through darker times, overcome struggles, and discovered the way to pull themselves out of this. It can be hard to realize the ways that you can pull yourself out of your pain as an individual, so it is important to recognize that you are able to learn how to do this from others who have already experienced the same things as you. Influencers will want a beneficial situation for everyone, not just themselves.

Influencers know that they will not be around forever, but they still care about making sure that the world is going to be a better place long after they're gone. This might be out of the goodness of their heart or they might just want to ensure that no one has to struggle in the same way that they did for the rest of their lives. Influencers will know how to listen to others. They understand that they're not perfect and will be more than willing to take advice from those around them. Influencers know that they don't have all the answers and that sometimes they will learn more about themselves from other people rather than thinking that they have all that they need on their own. They will recognize their flaws and do their best to change.

They will have the ability to admit that they are wrong and know that even if they are a pretty emotionally stable person, there is always going to be room for them to improve themselves. They will stay fluid with some of their beliefs to remain always willing to be critical of themselves and of others (Caprino, 2014).

<u>The Types of Mind Manipulators</u>

We already know that manipulators come in all different shapes and sizes. There are a few similar types that you should know the difference between. We never want to lump all people into one group, because when we do, there is a higher likelihood that we'll make too many assumptions. Whenever you start to assume too much about a person, this can lead to you overlooking important details that actually matter. However, knowing these similarities is only going to help you grow as a person. There are a few things that all manipulators have in common. These aren't necessarily patterns that have been learned, but rather, a mental solution in order to get the things that they might desire. Rather than being taught how to be manipulative, it can sometimes just be a simple pathway that their brain follows in order to try and help them get the things that they want the most from other people.

All manipulators will usually look for your greatest weakness to use against you. They will figure out what your biggest insecurity is and try to find ways to use that in order to gain power over you. They might try and discover what it is that you are bad at so that they can emphasize this trait in you and make you feel like you are a bad person overall because of this. They will often talk about your weaknesses and your flaws and make sure to point them out to others whenever they can in an attempt to humiliate you. Once they are able to do this, it becomes much easier to exert power over you. They will often try to start competitions with you.

Even in the smallest things that require absolutely no competition whatsoever, they will look for ways that they can prove themselves and "win." With a manipulator, an argument will never be something that helps both people grow and learn. Instead, it will only be a way for the manipulator to prove how much smarter they might be. They can go through life acting as if everything is a competition. Often, you might not even realize just how competitive someone else is or that they are constantly competing with you in their minds. You might bring something up as an accomplishment, and rather than being happy for you, they might point out a way in which they are better than you because of an equal or greater accomplishment that they have. They will use your words against you as well.

A manipulator is going to be really good at hanging onto every last word that leaves your mouth, and they will look for their chance to pull this out at the most random and unrelated times in order to prove their point and exert their power over you. Guilt is a great tactic as well. They will try their best to make sure that you are feeling really terrible about a situation that they might have caused! They will find a way to make you feel guilty over your own emotions. Sometimes we might react in ways that aren't the healthiest, but we should never be ashamed of the emotion that we felt behind that reaction in the first place. They will be absorbed with their own perspective and unwilling to see things from anyone else's point of view. They will have created their own world in their own minds that only serves them. If someone else tries to break through the walls of the world and expose it to the truth, the manipulator will completely shut down and protect their ideologies like soldiers defending their homes.

There is no getting through to manipulative people, and those manipulators that do manage to find the strength to realize the fault in their ways will usually make this discovery on their own. Some emotional manipulation will be very hard to see. There are some people who have been developing their manipulative tactics since they were teenagers, letting them become the definition of who they are. The longer that someone has been manipulating, the better they will be at hiding their overt manipulative tactics and making them seem less harmful. Other manipulation tactics will be more obviously violent. There might be some manipulators who use their physical strength to commit acts of violence that keep others subdued.

They might be able to simply puff their chest and use an aggressive face in order to keep others under their control. Within each of these categories, it gets a little more extreme the boundaries that they are willing to break and the lines they aren't afraid to cross. All manipulators will have more than one of these traits that we discussed. The level of how ingrained these are in their relationships and how violent they might be is what will really vary from person to person. Let's look at a few specific types of manipulators and the individual tactics they might use in an attempt to have control over other people.

Narcissist

Narcissists are the more common type of manipulators. They have created a world in which their own opinions, thoughts, and actions matter more than anyone else's. Often, narcissists come from abusive households themselves. When we're children, we have a fight or flight response, but we will not always have the ability to react in the way we would as adults. We can't fight because we're small kids, and parents have more physical force over us. We can't flee because again, we're kids, and there's nowhere for us to really go other than in our parental guardian's care. As a response to this, we still manage to "flee" into our brains, isolating ourselves within a world of protection that we created.

Narcissistic tendencies will start to form as we get older as a response to the constant escape to this fantasy world that we have created in our minds. In this fantasy world, we live in a protected boundary with thick walls that we keep up in order to prevent others from getting in. In this world, we are protected, which means that the ego can't be disturbed. This is why narcissists will have trouble admitting they are wrong and seeing things from the perspective of anyone other than themselves. Narcissists need a ton of attention. They have to have the center of the focus be on them at all times. When it is not on them, they will completely shut down. They will only be thinking of themselves, and the constant attention is needed in order to serve that little child that still sits protected behind the walls that they have built. Narcissists will struggle to have empathy for anyone else.

Their own problems have become so inflated that they can't imagine that anyone else is struggling as much as they might be. Rather than listening to other people and the experiences that others' might have had, narcissists will only care to share their own feelings. If you are talking to a narcissist about your problems, you will find that they will turn it around on themselves.

You might say something like, "I've been feeling depressed lately." A healthy response is, "I'm sorry you are experiencing that, what can I do to help you through this?" A narcissist might say something like, "I'm depressed too," and carry on to talking about their own struggles. They will not look at a conversation as a way to interact with someone else; it will only be a way for them to start a conversation about themselves.

They will believe that they are the most important at the time. They might know they're not perfect, but rather than admitting that they can work on things themselves, they will blame their shortcomings on other things and other people. For example, if someone failed a test, they might tell others, "I really didn't understand that part of the test, but I also have to admit that I could have studied more." A narcissist will say something like, "The teacher of the class is terrible, and I couldn't focus because of the things that they did," while giving many other excuses. Narcissists often have big ideas and will frequently fantasize about their success. They will envision a time in their lives when everything will turn out well for them rather than actively trying to work and grow toward this goal. They think they are special and beyond comparison with most people, with the exception of those that they also believe to be special and important. A narcissist will honestly believe that they are better than most people. When they do have people that they can look up to, they will idolize these people and think that they can do no wrong.

Narcissists will likely have trouble being happy for anyone else. They will feel an intense amount of jealousy and do whatever they can to try and bring the other person down because of their successes. Narcissists often feel as though they are owed something (Kassel, 2019). Of course, we are all owed our basic human rights. However, narcissists will still believe that they deserve special treatment above anyone else. They think that no one but them is deserving of the greatness that they want everyone else to give to them.

Psychopath and Sociopath

Sociopathy is commonly associated with being a psychopath. The two are different, however, and psychopaths share some characteristics with sociopaths, but they are certainly more extreme than sociopaths. This is really the darkest part of dark psychology. Most serial killers, murderers, rapists, and the worst abusers ever will either be a psychopath or sociopath. This is some of the strangest human behavior, especially because it is something that we can't recognize at all within other animals. Humans are the only animals that seem to kill and torture others just for sheer pleasure. Psychopaths and sociopaths are both very aggressive. They believe that violence is a great way to get the things that they desire.

They don't care whatsoever about inflicting pain on other people, which is why many will be so violent toward other people. They will not really be concerned with their image. A narcissist is going to be more worried about keeping up appearances and making sure that they are presented in a certain light, whereas a psychopath or sociopath isn't afraid to let their dark side show to others. Of course, the most skilled psychos of the world will be able to keep themselves looking good on the outside. Think of serial killers like Jeffrey Dahmer and the BTK killer who lived regular lives up until the moment that they were caught.

However, many other psycho and sociopaths will not be afraid to yell and scream at a group of people if it means that they will get what they want/exert their power. They have almost no boundaries and rarely show respect. Even if you blatantly ask them to stop, they will push the boundaries forward. Rather than really listening to the wants and desires of someone else and creating and maintaining healthy boundaries, they will create their own limits and force others to follow these rules. They will not feel sorry for the things that they did either. They might say "sorry," but they will never actually mean the words that come out of their mouths. They have little remorse because they lack empathy.

<u>Those Who Are Commonly Influenced</u>

It is not your fault that you have been manipulated. If you are someone who has found yourself in multiple relationships with manipulators, you are not alone. Manipulators will commonly look for certain types of people in order to serve their own needs. You will rarely discover a close relationship between two manipulators because both will struggle to have the upper hand in the relationship. Sometimes we have certain traits that make us more susceptible to being a victim of this abuse. You are not at fault for this, and you should never allow yourself to take the blame for the abuse that you have experienced. There are still certain things that people will look for when choosing a target.

Manipulators want people who are more passive. They are looking for individuals who would rather put up with what the manipulators say rather than trying to actively fight the manipulation that the manipulators are attempting to enforce. People-pleasers and those who are highly sensitive to emotions will likely find themselves being desired by those who are skilled manipulators. Sometimes it is simply our status they were after first. Manipulators might target those who have money or more status because they simply want that as well. Every so often there seems to be some story about how a celebrity might be dating someone who is only interested in the relationship because of the celebrity's fame.

You'll hear the celebrity tell stories of the goodness of this person and how it is true love. This can be the case, but every so often, we might wonder if they are actually being a manipulative individual who is using this person to get the things that they want. Those who are codependent might find that they want to help narcissists. They have a deep need inside of them to help others. Those who are codependent create their identity around being compassionate and providing other people with the help they need. They might actively seek out people they will be able to help and serve just to fulfill a need within themselves. You might have low self-esteem and often be the first one to take the blame for a situation. If you are someone who constantly says "sorry" for things that aren't even remotely your fault, beware because this can be a trait that manipulators desire.

They want people who are going to be harder on themselves because it will be easier for the manipulators to validate that negative voice within their victims. Those who are passive and people-pleasers are more likely to fall victim to manipulators. None of these traits are necessarily something you should feel bad about. It is just important that we're aware of how they affect our interactions with others so that we can better protect ourselves in the future.

Symptoms of Dark Psychology

In order to really understand the way that this negative manipulation has affected your life, it's crucial that we become aware of the way that this kind of emotional abuse might have rewired our brain and the way that we perceive ourselves and the world. Throughout this section, we are going to go over a long list of both everything small that others might have used against you and everything big that might have really transformed the way that you think. Manipulators are really good at getting inside of your head and switching up the way your brain operates, so it's crucial now that we better understand what this looks like in our own heads so we can reverse our thoughts and live a happier and healthier life. A common form of manipulation is the use of humiliation in victims.

Manipulators will ridicule, mock, and judge their victims in order to ensure that the manipulators themselves are the ones looking the best. They will go very deep with their jokes and are not afraid to hurt your feelings. All that matters is that you are the butt of the joke. What this does to you is make you feel as though you are an embarrassment. You will be ashamed of certain aspects of your life, and it can make you very self-conscious in front of other people. Rather than dealing with real issues that you have with yourself, you might find it's simply easier to close yourself off so that you don't experience more hurt and pain from other people. If you are someone who has experienced emotional abuse, then there is a very good chance that you will hear this person's voice in the back of your head.

When you are feeling embarrassed or slightly ashamed, theirs is likely the first voice that pops into your head. You might consider what they would think if they saw you, and they will have you feeling guilty over your actions even when they aren't aware of the things that you have done. They have managed to slip into your head, and it can be incredibly challenging to get them out. You might find that you are even at the point where you are terrified of them or what they might do to you, especially if they were to find out the embarrassing or shameful thing that you did. You might discover that you are someone who is always saying "sorry" or apologizing for things that you don't even have any part in. This is because the abuser shamed you for some time and always placed the blame on you.

You will be filled with regret and remorse over things that you have absolutely no control over, all because you were made to feel as though everything was your fault. You will feel guilt and agony over things far beyond your individual reach, and you may go as far as to feel guilty for large political and social issues all because you feel ashamed of even your smallest actions. You might discover that you have become a passive person who is no longer able to stick up for themselves. Even with interactions outside of your manipulator's presence, you might discover that it's best for you to just sit quietly and not participate in the conversation because you are too fearful or it brings about too much anxiety in general for you to feel comfortable speaking your truth and standing up for yourself.

They will make you feel isolated and like there is no one that you can relate to, all so that it is easier for them to have control over you. They gaslighted you for so long and made you feel as though what you had to share had no value, so it will be even more challenging for you to stand up for yourself and say what's on your mind now. On some level, you might have even found that you are interwoven with their problems and that you have become codependent on taking care of them. This is dangerous because even after you might end the relationship, you could still be deeply devoted to this person and feel frequent pain and anxiety when you cannot be there to take care of them.

Codependency involves one person who might need help and aide in some way, and the other person needing to help them. It is often seen in parent-child relationships and with those who care for individuals with disabilities. You no longer feel the need to take care of yourself because someone has stripped away your own identity. In response, you now take on the role of caretaker for the other person in order to find fulfillment. It can frequently go unnoticed, but once you do discover again that you might have this issue, it can be rather damaging.

Chapter 3 : Dark Psychology Trait

Now that you recognize what a manipulator is, you can start to better understand some of the actual tactics that they use. It can be easier for some to start to understand what makes up a manipulator and the common signs that are easy to spot. What is it that they actually do in order to gain power, however? What methods are they going to be working with that will keep us trapped under their control for all this time? Everyone will have their own methods of exerting control over other people. It will be dependent on the naturally powerful aspects they already have, along with the status that they hold in life.

These tactics will become part of their personality and will be the way that they are naturally used to reacting to different situations. Remember to not let these signals cause paranoia. Doing something once does not mean they're manipulative. Sometimes we might panic, and this could cause us to feel as though we need to do something quick to try and gain control over a situation. When we react off of our instincts, it can sometimes be because we aren't always thinking clearly, so maybe there's the chance that you've done something slightly manipulative in the past. You are looking for a pattern of manipulative behavior.

It's not just once instance of manipulation that should make you feel as though you need to run from a person who tries to be controlling. What you need to be more cautious of is a pattern of behavior that another person seems to have. If they are doing these things on a consistent basis, then it means that there's a good chance they'll have more manipulative tendencies. The biggest red flag is if this pattern keeps happening and there is no effort from them or even acknowledgment that they should try and change the way that they handle their emotions.

Sometimes this requires stepping outside the boundaries of how you might judge someone and viewing it from a bird's eye perspective. It can be hard to see all of the restrictions of manipulation when you are already trapped in the web. Try and picture if you were the person outside of a manipulative relationship. How would you view it compared to how others might? If you were sharing this experience with someone else and trying to describe it like you would the plot of a movie, how would it sound? Simplify it as much as possible and allow yourself some perspective so you can discover if you are really in a manipulative relationship or not.

Remember that you shouldn't be using these tactics to take advantage of anyone else. These are just methods that you can become aware of so if you feel as though someone is manipulating you, you will know how to escape from it. You have to come from a place of deep hurt and negligence to do this to someone else. Whatever pain you inflict on others is also pain that you might end up feeling yourself. Always ask what the manipulator might want out of this situation. If there is something at stake, they could be manipulating you.

Whenever you're not sure if you're paranoid about being manipulated or if you actually are being manipulated, always ask what their true intention is. If you can't figure out why they might be trying to control you, then they just might be doing so in order to gain power over you.

Body Language of Manipulators

Unfortunately, not everyone is going to have a big warning sign with them letting you know that they're going to try and manipulate you. If the world's biggest manipulators did have these warning signs, we'd be a lot better off. We would be able to walk away before falling into their manipulative tactics. It's so crucial that we start to pick up on the actual body language and tactics of these manipulators now rather than later. We can still remove ourselves and recover, but remember that it's always going to be easier to not have to deal with it at all. It's better to prevent getting a disease rather than having to try and cure it, so always look for ways to avoid these manipulators now.

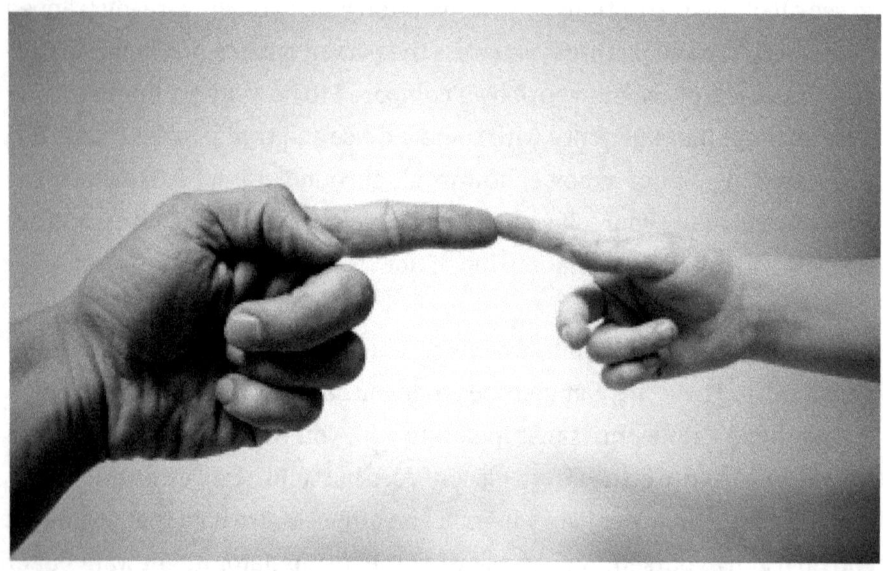

One way that we can pay attention to how someone might end up treating us is by picking up on their overall body language. Listening to the words that they share and the thoughts that they have is really important, but you also have to ensure that you can pick up on the different kinds of body language that they use. The things that they do with their eyebrows all the way down to their feet can give you so much insight that you never would have noticed had you not made yourself first aware of this kind of language. Some of it might be intentional, but there are other instances where it's entirely subconscious as well. It might be a way to try and persuade you to do something, a type of body movement to make you more comfortable around them so you open up, or a way to physically scare you with their bodily movements.

Manipulators at first will keep themselves closed off. They will want to read you and understand who you are. They might be cryptic with what they say, but then you will also start to notice that they hold their bodies closed off as well. They might have their arms crossed or their body language turned away from you. Look at their jaw and the way that they are holding their faces. If they are tense and closed off, it might give you the idea that they are keeping things from you. They can keep their mouths closed as well. Sometimes, they might even hold their hand over their mouth. Pay attention to if they make a fist and keep it clenched over the bottom half of their faces. This could be a sign that they are trying to hide something from you or keeping themselves from saying something that they actually want to share.

Sometimes tight lips can do this as well. They might try to make themselves bigger, which is why you'll sometimes hear people describe aggressors as "puffing their chests." They might stand up even though everyone else is sitting down. If they are standing frequently and making themselves as tall as possible, then they might put their hands on their hips as well. They might stand in a wide stance with their feet farther than shoulder-width apart. They might also sit this way, with their knees spread apart trying to take up as much space as possible. Again, some of these body language signals might be a sign that they are just feeling anxious. If they're feeling self-conscious you should look at the way they might be closing themselves off with crossed arms or by holding a pillow on their lap to keep themselves blocked off. The thing you will always have to ask yourself is whether they are trying to increase their confidence or trying to exert themselves over everyone in the room.

Matching Body Language

It is not uncommon for us to match the same body language as those that we might be talking to. Sometimes it happens naturally without even thinking about it. How often have you found that you picked up on the smaller habits that other people have? Maybe they have a certain catchphrase or laugh in a specific way. Sometimes we just do this naturally, but look out for people who do this quickly or in a way that makes you feel a little suspicious. If someone is already saying your catchphrases after just a few hours of hanging out, then they might be intentionally trying to match your body language or behavior. A manipulator is going to use this tactic, and they are going to take it way over the top. If you turn your head to the side while talking, they might turn theirs as well. If you take a sip of your water, so might they. If you get up and move around, they might as well. It will be natural for others to want to turn themselves toward you so they can better hear the things you have to say.

However, if their body language is constantly mimicking yours, then be careful about whether or not they're trying to manipulate you. Like everything else we discussed, it's going to be a pattern of behavior. It's not just going to be one instance of mimicking or only done at times that make sense. It will be a constant attempt to try and do the same things that you are doing. This is because they want you to feel more open with them. They want to make you feel as though the two of you can share everything together. This is an attempt to be more relatable. If you really want to see whether or not they are being vindictive or doing it intentionally, start to change your body language. If they are matching and mimicking everything that you do, then it will be easier to notice this tactic in others.

Frequent Staring

Those that aren't fully listening to you will try to overly stare. Rather than actually engaging with what you're saying and staring at you to get a better comprehension of what you're saying, some manipulators will instead try to convince you that they're listening. They might be planning what they are going to say next, especially if you are in the middle of an argument. Then, rather than actually taking in what you are saying, they will think to themselves, "Keep eye contact so they know you're engaged." Sometimes this staring is even a way to intimidate you. They might use their glare to make sure that you know that they're watching you. They might overly emphasize that they are looking at you and actually turn their entire body in order to direct it right at you. This is a method that they can then use in order to make you feel like they have more power over you. They might make a face with their eyes but then tell you that you are crazy if you call them out for it.

Manipulators are really good at keeping their brow straight in order to give you a direct glare. They will squint their eyes or make a grimacing face. If you ask something like, "What's wrong? Why are you making that face," they will reply with something like, "This is just my face." They will find a way to act as though they aren't giving you a weird look in order to make it seem as though you are misinterpreting the scenario and thinking too deeply about something that isn't true. They will often be thinking about what to say next rather than actually listening to the things that you are sharing. All of these methods are easily picked up on if you start to really look at the way that they are looking at you. Either too much or not enough eye contact could be a sign that they're not fully engaged. Some people really have trouble making eye contact, and others will be anxiously thinking in their head, so they might try harder to make eye contact. Just look out for shady eyes and shifty patterns that might indicate they are attempting to gain control over you.

Quick Talking and Hand Movements

Manipulators will make sure that they talk with their hands and as fast as they can. These are two methods that you will notice frequently if someone is trying to convince you to do something. This is an especially common tactic if they want to convince you of something that will clearly be harder to push you over the edge on. They will want to urge you to agree because they know if you're given too long to decide, you will easily spot the weak points in the plan. They'll talk fast so that you will not even be able to pick up on all the little things they might be saying. They might want to slip something in that you don't notice, but they still state it so that you can't say that they didn't warn you afterward. Think of the last commercial that you watched for a medication. They'll start saying all of the amazing benefits that their products provide, but then they will also slip in the warnings and side effects at the end of the commercial.

The beginning will include dramatizations or "customer" interviews selling the medicine for you with pretty pictures and grand promises. After they've done this, the commercial ends with a speed talker stating scary things like, "This medicine may cause internal bleeding, bone loss, skin lesions, random hair growth, and could make your current side effects even worse." Make sure to always listen to all the fast talk you hear because you never know what scary warnings might be hidden within them. Manipulators will also try to overstate their point by using hand movements. This is something that you will see with a lot of salespeople or those who are at least trying to be persuasive in minor negative ways. They will really talk up their point and try to prove what they're stating using grand gestures and wide or rapid hand movements. It's almost like they are the conductor of an orchestra trying to make sure that everyone is following their lead. This isn't as bad of a tactic because some people will just be more vivid storytellers who overdo the hand gestures. Just be cautious of this method especially when in a position where someone is trying to sell you a product or service.

Persuasion Tactics Used

If you are not sure whether or not you are being persuaded, always remember to question what the intention of this conversation might be. They might have every sign of being a manipulator, but are they actually trying to control you, or do they just want what's best for you? Sometimes people really do know certain things that we might need in our lives, maybe like a parent or a spouse. Just because they are going against what you're saying and have an idea for what you should do instead doesn't mean they're being manipulative. Always consider if it's just in this instant, or if it's natural for others to try and control you. There are still a few more methods of persuasion that we'll be discussing in order to help you become more aware of the embedded manipulative tactics others have used on you.

When manipulative people are mad, they might end up giving you the silent treatment. They will completely shut out and not give you a chance to talk. It is sort of like a "strike" from the relationship. They might think that if they completely cut you out of their life, they'll be able to scare you into running back and apologizing, accepting responsibility even if they were the ones to do something negative in the first place. It is a cold and calculated move that can really hurt the other person. They won't usually last that long, however. The thing is, the other person, the non-manipulator, will usually be the one to reach out because they are compassionate and empathetic, and it legitimately hurts them to try and go without the other person in their life.

Next time someone gives you the silent treatment, let them go quiet. They will eventually come back to you. If they don't, then that's not a healthy person to have in your life anyway. Sometimes people need space, but they should let you know that first. It shouldn't just be an attempt to cut someone out of their life cold turkey. They might try and take you to their "home court." This is a manipulative tactic that's frequently done by salesmen and other individuals trying to close a deal. It will involve bringing someone to a place where the person in control is more comfortable. This is done on a personal level as well. Maybe a partner wants to have a "talk," but they choose to only do so at their house or even in their car where they can be the one driving.

If someone is being very adamant about having a discussion only in their own personal space, then this might be a sign they are trying to gain the upper hand. They will not really give you much of a chance to talk. They want to take the lead in this conversation and interaction. They need to have the upper hand, which means that they will end up doing as much of the talking as possible. If you find that someone is frequently interrupting you, make sure that you ask them, "Can I finish speaking please?" Don't try to cut them off if they don't let you finish every time. Give them a minute and then allow a moment of silence to show that you are being as respectful as possible. They might realize just how much they aren't letting you talk at this moment, but they could also end up just interrupting you again.

If the interruption continues and your efforts to speak aren't working, you can remove yourself from the situation and give them a chance to calm down. It will be better to have a serious discussion when both parties are willing to be active listeners. They'll belittle you and make you feel as though you aren't very intelligent. They will ask things like, "did you really just say that?" or call you names like "stupid" and "dumb." They will make you feel as though you aren't intelligent enough to make your own decisions and look for ways to insult your intellect with passive-aggressive comments. Pressure and time-pressing issues might be a way that they want to control you.

This is another method that many advertisers will use in order to sell their products. They'll say things like, "this offer won't last" or "limited supplies," in order to make you think that you are missing out on a once in a lifetime opportunity. Here are some more complex issues that you can start to understand in order to determine whether or not you are being persuaded.

Using Your Emotions Against You

Manipulators will know your biggest fears. They are very skilled at picking out your greatest weaknesses, and they will also be conscious of the things you are good at as well. They view many things through the lens of competition, so it will be common to know what you are good and bad at. Rather than trying to match skills and compete on a fair level, they will jab you in all of your weakest areas. Manipulators aren't afraid to play dirty. Once they are aware of your biggest weaknesses, they will take any opportunity they get to make sure that you are being exploited in these areas. They will see that you are happy, and they will take advantage of this as well. They will wait until you're in a good mood to ask for a favor.

They will break the bad news to you only after cooking you dinner or giving you a gift. This isn't a totally terrible method to ask others for favors and such; however, they should be doing nice things for you all of the time and not just when they need something from you. If you are feeling low or depressed, then they are going to help to ensure that you feel even worse. They might take advantage of this moment and use it to validate a feeling.

For example, imagine a couple that includes a boyfriend and a girlfriend. The girlfriend decides to go back to school to get a new degree. The boyfriend doesn't like this because it means that she won't be home as often to help take care of him, and his insecurities start to emerge surrounding her success and intelligence. He gets scared that she will meet new a partner at school and leave him once she improves her life like she wants to. She comes home from class one day and is upset because she failed a test. A healthy relationship would involve the boyfriend telling her that everything was going to be OK and that she shouldn't let one test stop her from achieving her dreams. In this relationship, the boy is manipulative, so he tells her that this is a sign that maybe she should drop out. He will use it to validate his negative perspective.

Charming and Love Bombing

A manipulator knows exactly what to tell you. They will be masters at flirtation and know exactly the right things to say that you want to hear from them. They will have several different cheesy lines they might be able to recite, and they will often use the same phrases among different people in order to charm them. They have perfect lines that come out so smoothly. This is because they will often play out scenes in their head before actually living through them. As we've already discussed, they believe their own lies. It will be harder to catch them in these lies or call them out for being phony because they've already come up with lines of defense in their own minds. They will want to get that same treatment back from you.

They might overload you with love and gifts because they are expecting the same treatment in return. They might do these favors and then one day throw them back in your face when it comes time for you to do a favor for them. They will not do this for other people. This is especially true for a romantic relationship. If you are noticing that they're very loving to you but rude to your friends, family, and even their friends, it's a good sign that they're phony. Genuinely charming people will be like that with most others, not just with the person that they want to manipulate.

Oversharing Then Reverse

There are a few phases that a manipulator will go through in order to try and win you over. At first, during the love-bombing phase, they will get you to tell them a lot about yourself. This is where they will act as though they are a therapist just there to listen to everything that you have to say and give you basic comments to help make you feel better.

hey are then going to overshare with you as well. Everything that you went through they totally understand. If you lost a parent, so did they, and they know exactly what that felt like. If you were bullied in high school, so were they. They will look for every way to relate to you and go as far as to lie about their life in order to make it seem like the two of you are meant to be together. They know just the right things to say in order to ensure that you are listening to them. During this phase, they are going to take everything about you and save it to eventually use against you. They will get you to open up so that it's easier to stab you right in the heart! That's a little dramatic, but it is a genuine tactic that many manipulators can use. They will want to make you feel as though you can trust them and tell them anything all so that they can gather the ammo they need to come back at you later. They want to relate to you more than anyone else so that they can start to keep you isolated from everyone else. They will start to make you feel like your friends and family don't understand you and only they do. Don't be afraid of opening up to others, but ensure that you aren't blinded by someone who knows how to pretend as though they are good listeners.

Confusion and Un-Comfortability

Manipulators might push you past your boundaries but then make you feel bad if you bring this up. Manipulators will not care about what makes you uncomfortable or what doesn't. They will push you into situations that you are uncomfortable with and then get mad at you if you try to bring up how they hurt you. For example, let's think of two best friends. The first one, we'll call him Jim, decided to play a prank on his friend Sam. He took the prank a little too far and ended up really hurting Sam in the process. Maybe Jim played a prank that his dog died or someone broke into his house. Sam didn't think this was funny whatsoever, so he gets angry and takes some time away from Jim. Rather than being a reasonable friend and apologizing for what he did, Jim is a manipulator. He ends up getting mad that Sam couldn't handle the joke and gives him the silent treatment for several weeks.

You can see that he pushed passed Sam's boundaries and made it seem like Sam's fault that he was upset. You'll often find that after having an interaction with a manipulator, you might wind up thinking something like, "What on earth just happened?" They can stab you in the stomach with a smile on their face and somehow leave you as the one that does all the apologizing. "I was just joking" delivered in a passive-aggressive tone is a great way to make you feel as though you are in the wrong for being upset or sharing that you were hurt in a certain interaction. They might call you by different nicknames rather than what you actually want to be called (Fellizar, 2018). They won't be afraid to push your buttons because it is a way to entertain themselves and gain control over you.

NLP Tactics

NLP stands for neuro-linguistic programming. It is a way that we can start to understand the methods in which we communicate and how we can manipulate the way we talk with other people. N is for neuro. This is the way that our brains operate and the neural processing they go through when learning and applying different information. L is for linguistic. This is the language that you use in order to interact. P is for programming. It involves the way that we have been programmed to think in this world. A lot of the methods that we have discussed already are also neurolinguistics techniques in order to control you. These include:

- Bringing you to their home turf
- Talking fast and using large hand movements
- Matching body language Not all of these things are bad.

You can try these persuasive techniques yourself. It's just important that you are ensuring that you are persuading and influencing another person in a positive way that will mutually benefit both of you. Another popular NLP tactic is anchoring. This is basically weighing down an emotion so that it's easier to elicit later on. If they notice that you are in a particular mood, they might simply touch you. Then, if they want to elicit this mood later on, they will touch you in the exact same way. They might not do this with you physically, but with objects as well. Let's say you're discussing a business deal with someone skilled in NLP tactics.

At the beginning of the discussion, they put you in a happy mood ask how your family is or how your vacation was. At this time, when you're at your happiest, they might do something like tap the table twice with their fingers, a sort of natural nervous tick that goes mostly unnoticed. Later, as they're trying to really drive in the deal, they'll do this same tapping, bringing you back to that happy moment. Look out for those who seem to be experts trying to elicit these feelings. More individuals go out of their way to train with these NLP methods than you might think.

Chapter 4 : Reasons for Analyzing People

We should all have a certain level of social cognition that will enable us to better understand and help the people around us. Since we are group animals who need others to survive, it's important that we know how to fit into this world. That's not an easy thing to do, but it can still be helpful to our survival to meet other people like us and make deeper connections with those that we can relate to. When you use tactics to try and get a better understanding of how people operate, it makes it easier to predict what they might do or how they might act. Rather than trying to guess your way through this life, always wondering how other people are feeling, you can really start to take charge and better understand even the most complex people that you meet.

This will help you throughout your life, but it will also enable you to help others. We all have loved ones who might be struggling who we wish we could help more, but that can sometimes be difficult. If you start to analyze people and better grasp where it is that they're coming from, you're giving yourself the chance to look for ways that you can actually help them. There might actually be evolutionary purposes as to why it is that we, as humans, ensure that we can pick up and learn from the behavior of other people. A leopard doesn't teach its cub how to hunt by sitting it down and talking through the steps.

The best way that these animals learn is to start with something small and work their way up, all the time watching their parents do the killing first to give them an idea of how it works. These mirror brain methods of comprehension also help us to pick up valuable information just like the animals that watch others to learn. As we grow older, you can start to pick up on more of your surroundings. You often learn from the actions of those that teach you while you grow. It's important to understand all the ways that you learn about both yourself and other people when you sit down and really start to understand the many ways that the human brain really operates. You will be more in tune with various signals that help give you a better understanding overall rather than taking information at face value.

Many people will not actually say the things that are on their minds. Sometimes it is hard to express ourselves using only the words that we already know. We aren't always taught to express ourselves in healthy ways, so we might simply not know how to do that. There are situations where it can just be plain scary to open up and say what's on our minds. This difficulty in communication can lead to some very toxic and damaging relationships, so the better equipped we are to speak to one another, the easier it will be to navigate through life. When you can learn to pick up on both verbal and non-verbal cues, it becomes easier to understand the intention of what others actually desire. At first, you might still miss some signs of people manipulating you.

You might also realize that you are paranoid at times and looking too deep into signals that don't actually mean anything. Communication is a practice that not everyone will be perfect at, so don't feel discouraged if it takes a while to get used to understanding dark psychology. The more you learn to analyze and understand people, the easier it becomes to manipulate them as well. This is to be done in a positive and influential way, of course. Let's discuss more in-depth about why analyzing people can be important.

Why Use Manipulation?

Manipulation is an easy way to get people to do what you want. If you are someone with power, physical strength, or a lot of money, you are already equipped to be more influential. Here's the issue, however. You could boss people around, tell them what to do, and intimidate others into listening to you. This can be easily done depending on your status in life. However, none of these types of manipulation is going to be substantial enough to last. Eventually, many people will realize the control that is happening and will be less easily persuaded. Others will be afraid and want to escape. You'll no longer want to manipulate people for negative reasons. If you really want long-lasting influence, it has to be done in a positive way.

Others will be more influenced by you and have a greater level of respect when you are able to share a positive influence with them. If you are a highly aware individual, then you will be able to use your influence for good and help to change things to make the world a better place. An influencer is someone who strives to be more of an equal with the people they are persuading. You will have a time when communication can occur, and you can be open with the other person. This will allow both of you to grow, and even when you don't know if what you're doing is the best choice, you will have an open dialogue with others that will help to keep the group moving in the right direction. A manipulator will think that they know exactly what's best for everyone, and even if they realize they are wrong halfway through, they will still do their best to ensure that they prove their point.

You will actually learn a lot about yourself from what you learn from other people. Sometimes you really need an outsider's perspective to grasp the reality of the situation you are the center of. They might be able to help you be more aware of the situation, or they might have gone through something similar that gives you insight into your own scenario.

You can help to break through the boundaries that people might have not been so willing to change in the past. You can help to show a positive influence and the way that it can transform lives for the better, enabling healthy relationships to form between you and those that you are closest to. Manipulation will enable you to finally speak up for yourself and say what's on your mind. Rather than being a passive person who is afraid to stick up for themselves, you can be more willing to express your opinions, giving you the strength to stick up for yourself. You can start to get to know people on a deeper level as you tap into their subconscious beyond just what you've discussed in the past. It can be easy to get defensive and turn away from someone, but when you really dive deep into the "why" behind emotions, it can end up bringing you and the other person closer in the end. All of these reasons we discussed are why it is important that we learn how to use manipulation but in the positive form of persuasion.

How to Protect Yourself Against Persuasion

We all have times when we've been easily influenced by others. Maybe you accidentally signed up for something you never would have if you'd been given more time to think about it. Maybe someone even swindled you or tricked you into a deal that ended up leaving you with the short end of the stick. Don't feel bad if this has happened to you. It's time now to become much more aware of the way that we can protect ourselves in certain situations. Sometimes it is not so bad to let other people make decisions. It's nice every once in a while to have another person just make the decisions about what to watch on TV that night or what to eat for dinner. Not every night, of course, but there are some instances when we just might struggle to make decisions.

However, we should still always be as aware as possible of the ways in which we might be falling under someone else's persuasion. The first thing you can do to resist persuasion is to avoid the person trying to persuade you altogether. If you notice that they might be someone who is trying to trick you into doing something, then it's important to keep your guard up right away. Next, you can try to put up a defense. Make them question what they're trying to sell to you. If you really aren't sure whether or not you're being manipulated, always ask more questions. Make sure you know the who/what/why/when/where of everything that you might sign up for. Be highly aware of both the positives and the negatives. Ask "what's the catch?" whenever something seems too good to be true.

Make the manipulator face the truth so that they are exposed, and you are more protected. Ask for some time to think when you feel pressure in the situation. If they aren't willing to give you a second to think without a substantial reason for needing the urgency, then it's a sign they are trying to trick you. If someone says, "unfortunately, you don't have time," always ask, "why?" If they give you a valid reason, such as a time period is ending or there's a greater risk on the line, then, of course, act as you should. However, a lot of deals can wait at least until the next morning, so you really have time to think things through. Don't be afraid to say "no." It can be so hard to say "no" to certain people. Maybe they don't seem to take "no" for an answer, or perhaps they have been so kind and accommodating that you would feel guilty saying "no." Don't let this happen! No means no, and if you said it once, you shouldn't have to say it again. Don't let others shame you for saying "no!" One of the best ways to protect yourself is to be confident and assured in your own core values. This can be done by developing your levels of emotional intelligence.

Emotional Intelligence

It is crucial that we all can reach a certain level of emotional intelligence. Your IQ is your ability to think intellectually and logically. Your emotional intelligence (EQ) is based more around your abilities to understand and recognize the feelings and emotions of those around you. In order to have a high level of emotional intelligence, you need to be aware of what your emotions are and where they started to form. The first way to start to become more emotionally intelligent is to always ask "why." Why is it that you are sad? Angry? Jealous? Scared? When you have these more challenging emotions, always question where they came from and what purpose they are serving. Ensure that you are separating the emotion from the reaction. If you are angry, you can either react by being quiet or punching a wall.

The emotion is the same, but it is the reaction that is positive or negative. Being angry or sad, or any other challenging emotion is not a bad thing. It's when you don't think your reaction through that things can get tricky. Someone with a high EQ knows how to react to their emotions in a healthy way, whereas those with a low EQ often act only on impulses. Always question your emotions and make sure that you are really looking deep within yourself. Did this emotion develop in the past? Is it a thought process you were taught? Is it something newer that you have developed? Start to listen better to others as well. Really actively engage in what they are saying and don't just sit there and try to plan out what you are going to say next. Listen to their words and the subtext in between. Voice your opinion and be honest with your feelings.

As long as you are not hurting anyone in the process, you should always express how you are feeling. If you bottle up your emotions, then you will only hurt yourself mentally and physically down the line. Remember to view things objectively. Don't label everything as either "positive" or "negative." There is plenty in between, and you will be able to find both a good and bad side to most things if you look hard enough. Strive for this ambiguity rather than putting everything in one box or the other. Control your immediate reactions. Let yourself process your feelings for a moment before deciding to react. When you start to improve on this, it becomes that much easier to protect yourself from manipulation.

Symptoms of Brainwashing

After going through a period where you might have experienced emotional abuse, it is important that you realize all of the ways that this has affected you. To properly heal and move on, you need to know how this has altered the way that you think. Long-term manipulation can be especially embedded in our psyche. It can be challenging to break free from some of the thoughts and words that our abusers put in our heads in the first place. Those who have been brainwashed will believe that the person who has done the manipulation is the only judge of their worth.

Many people who have been rescued from cults are still afraid of what their leaders might think, all because their values have become based on a scale that they were taught by their manipulator. If you are highly unsure of yourself and always wonder what the person who might have brainwashed you would say, then this is a good sign they emotionally manipulated you. If you can hear their voice in the back of your head, they have successfully brainwashed you, and it is time to start ignoring that voice, or at least trying to resist it. If you have experienced public shame from someone, then they likely played a role in brainwashing you.

They tried to exert power over you in a public setting, and this can really damage your self-worth. You might have become isolated from those who you used to be close with because of this person. Your friends and family might have tried to help, but your manipulator likely told you that they were all against you. Perhaps you feel guilty and like you could have helped your manipulator more. This is a sign that you are brainwashed because you are putting the responsibility of their life in your hands and convincing yourself that you could have changed the way things ended up.

Maybe you have been taught to fear outsiders or even the beliefs of others that don't align with what your manipulator taught you. If the emotional manipulator denies that they have hurt you in any way, this is a good sign that you need to separate yourself from this situation. Don't worry, your mental journey does not stop here. The first part of the book has concluded, and now it is time to get to the "how" of all of this! How are you going to use your new knowledge of manipulation in order to benefit you?

Chapter 5: The Art of Manipulation and Persuasion

Manipulation is the dark side of persuasion. We aren't going to tell you how to be manipulative because that's not going to do the world any good. You might be able to get what you want, but you would hurt people along the way. Nothing worth something substantial is going to be gained by taking from other people first. If you really want long-lasting influence, you have to start to gain ways that you can be more of a positively persuasive person. Don't persuade individuals who aren't going to be able to know any better. If someone isn't very intelligent and truly has trouble understanding basic concepts, then it's not a good idea to try and manipulate them.

You should only help inspire others to think the things they would be able to on their own, just with a little guidance. To inspire someone is to give them a good idea that influences their own thinking patterns. It doesn't involve planting an idea in their head and tricking them into thinking something they wouldn't ever have thought on their own. Never persuade someone to do something that you wouldn't do yourself, if in the same situation. If you aren't willing to do it, then it's a safe bet that it's not morally right to expect someone else to do it either.

Persuasion should not involve you taking from the other person. You shouldn't take something from them that leaves them with nothing. If you do take from them, then you should be giving them something of equal or greater value in the process. It is a shared experience that helps both of you become better people in the end. There should always be a sense of freedom felt by the other person. Think of it like you would if you were to find a lightning bug in a glass jar. You could put a lid on the jar and keep that lightning bug for your enjoyment. Or you could help the bug and set it free. If you keep it in the jar, it will eventually die, but if you set it free in the world, it will go wherever it pleases. You can still help people by giving them their own freedom to make decisions that are best for themselves. First, let's look at the frequent lies and deceptive tactics that you should avoid using at all costs and some other reminders of how you might have been manipulated in the past.

Deception and Lies

It is important that you are never deceptive on your journey of persuasion. The moment that you start trying to trick people into thinking something other than reality is when you become negatively persuasive. Lying is tricky. You could do it if you really wanted to, but with every lie, there is a truth. The lie could be long-lasting, but the truth will always remain just as long as the lie. It is only a matter of time until the lie is eventually discovered—if it doesn't eat away at you first. You don't want to try and convince others of anything that is untrue. You should be cautious of the other ways that could be considered lying.

Withholding the truth can sometimes be considered lying if you are intention-ally keeping secrets in order to persuade the other person. Of course, there will always be things that not everyone necessarily needs to know. If you were staying in a hotel room, you wouldn't really want to know what everyone has ever done in that room. It would probably be more important for you to know if that room has bed bugs, however! If what you are withholding from the other person could negatively affect them, then it's safe to say that you should share the truth. It is pretty easy to lie! For example, one of these is a lie. Pick out which one you think it is:

- A whale's heartbeat can be heard when you're within a two-mile radius.
- There are over 2,500 squirrels that live in Central Park.
- Coca-Cola used to contain cocaine.

Which one do you think it is? Guess what? All of these are true. The actual lie that was stated was that "one of these is a lie." It is just that easy to lie! You can do it whenever you want, at any time. The thing is, you won't always get away with it. If you don't get away with it, then you are going to cause more problems than what you might have had in the beginning when you initially chose to state the lie. Is lying always wrong? That's for you to decide. Is it wrong to lie to a toddler about their pet cat getting run over by the neighbor's car? Is it wrong to lie to a customer about how good they look in a dress so you can make a sale? Is it wrong to lie to your spouse about cheating after you already broke things off with your mistress? We all might have different opinions about these.

Maybe you think all are fine; maybe you think all are awful. Either way, they are common, and they are real, and we need to look out for these lies. There are some common signs that someone is lying, and you need to be aware of these signs. First, look at the way that they are talking. Are they stuttering? Stuttering is a nervous tick that we can have, especially in highpressure situations. Look at how someone might be stuttering or tripping over their words. If they are simply having trouble finishing a sentence, they might be nervous. If they struggle to keep up with the story and go off on too many over-explained tangents, they might be lying or at least bending the truth in their favor. How long is it taking them to answer?

This could indicate two different kinds of lies. If they take way too long, then they are thinking of the best way to respond that makes them look good. If they don't take long enough and answer really fast immediately after being asked, then they might have these answers already perfectly planned out. Look at what is being asked to determine whether or not they might be lying. Are they seemingly nervous in their movement? Fidgeting, shaking legs, and playing with their fingers can be nervous ticks but adding them to sweating, shifty eyes, and frequent swallowing could indicate that they are lying. If they are too still and incredibly tense, then this might also mean that they are doing their best to stay composed.

New manipulators who are still practicing their methods will likely be the ones to take too long to answer and be nervous and shifting. Skillful manipulators will be very still, collected, and ready with the perfect answer to all questions. If they seem to look off to the right, then this might be a sign that they're lying. This is because the left side of your brain is in control of logic, and the right side is in charge of creativity. If you look at the left side, this means your brain is using the memory reasoning aspects of your brain, and you might be trying to recall details. You are using logic to help you remember the answer. If you look to the right, you are tapping into your creative side. You are trying to come up with excuses and lies in order to cover yourself. If they are covering their mouths, then it might be a sign that they are attempting to withhold information. Trust your gut if you really think people are lying. Be careful if you decide to call others out. You don't want to accuse someone and have them end up losing your trust in the process.

<u>Mind Control and Brainwashing</u>

The difference between mind control and brainwashing is what your intentions are going to be. When you are brainwashing, you are wiping their head clean of everything that they might want to think on their own. You are trying to take their own thoughts and ideas away and instead replace them with your own. This is malicious intent. Mind control is a little better, as you will still be able to help influence the way that they think, but you will not do it in a way that limits their own freedom. There are a few mind control tactics you can use for good. The first tactic you can use is the amplification method. This involves highlighting the best parts of something and really running with that. To be honest, you should always make sure everyone is aware of the negative aspects.

However, an amplification tactic can help others to get really excited about the smaller details of a project. If a company is rebranding, they might come up with a new catchphrase and let this become their point of selling. Maybe it's an image or a phrase that helps you to best remember the new products that they have created. You can also make things seem scarcer. You might limit yourself or the things that you are trying to sell in order to make them more popular. Others will want to take advantage of the limited options in order to alleviate any fear they might have later over not following through with the purchase.

Point out legitimate compliments that go beyond just the basic ones that others are used to hearing. Don't tell someone that you like their shoes. Tell them that they have a great style! Don't say, "That's a good idea." Instead, try something like, "You have a really great ability to come up with new ideas." Give them more substantial compliments besides what is frequently said in order to give yourself a little advantage. Go out of your way to do something nice for others–but don't accept anything in return at first. You'll want to show that you legitimately care and appreciate them, and you aren't just doing nice things to get something from them. Help others to see the reason that there needs to be some action right now. Give them your perspective and remember to use objective phrasing rather than something that sounds more forceful.

Don't say, "You should do this." Instead, say, "I feel as though doing this has helped me, so you might find it does the same for you if you try." Others want to think that they are coming up with all of their own ideas; they're not always going to be so keen to take on all the thoughts that you have. Use logic and science to back up your argument. If I told you that 80 percent of people who read this sentence believed I didn't make this sentence up, would you be more compelled to believe it? Of course, there's no way of knowing that it's true, but facts and numbers are going to help more people be willing to believe the ideas that you're sharing. Remember the small details about other people. Ask about their family, remember their pet's name, discuss their interests, and so on. In order to better remember, associate that trait with something about them.

For example, maybe your employee's husband's name is Ray, and he just got out of the hospital after surgery, which is why your employee, Susan, had to take a few days off. Remember that R ay is her husband because she has R ed hair. Associating the two R's with Susan will help you to remember more. Then, when she comes back, make sure to not just ask, "How's your husband?" Instead, ask her, "Is Ray glad to be back home?" It's so much more personal and shows that you legitimately care and aren't just asking to be nice. Be flexible in the way that you are asking for things. If you show that you are angry, they didn't agree at first or are unwilling to compromise, that will be the first turn-off for the other person.

Negotiation is all about letting both parties have a say so that everyone comes out of it feeling happy and comfortable with the decisions that they've made. Always show positivity and enthusiasm. If you can't be excited about your own persuasion, why should anyone else? Have backup plans for what you might be trying to persuade others of. Not everyone is going to say "yes," and the most detail-oriented plans we have can still go in completely opposite ways. Be prepared for what you might do when everyone turns down your offers. Put yourself in their shoes so you will understand the things that might be red flags for them. Envision why they might just say no, not just what you will do if that's the way things go. If you can walk in someone else's shoes, you will better enable yourself to understand exactly where they're coming from.

Understanding Body Language

The first thing you will want to do when reading someone's body language is to remember the context that you are in. If you're giving an interview to a potential new employee, then, of course, they are going to be nervous. If you're interrogating a husband for the murder of his wife, then he is going to be nervous, but he's also more likely to be a manipulator than the person in the first example. The context is going to help reveal whether or not you should really have your guard up to protect against potential manipulators.

Look at the way that someone is holding their body. Are their arms crossed? Are they closed off? Rigid? Shaking? Start by taking in their overall stance first, and then you will be able to better understand the actual message they might be trying to show with their body language. Their posture and the way that they are positioned can give you an idea as to what they're saying through their bodies. What is their smile like? Squinted eyes and wrinkled cheeks will show that it is a genuine smile. Eyes that stay the same and cheeks that barely move is a good sign that they are just faking the smile. Their eyebrows will also reveal a lot about whether or not they are genuinely smiling. Raised eyebrows can mean that they are really excited about something, whereas turned in eyebrows with a smile could mean that they are happy but still questioning what is going on.

Straight and unchanged eyebrows are usually a sign that the smile is fake. Pay attention to the way that they are nodding. Not everyone will realize it, but sometimes when we're saying "yes/no" while also lying, our heads can actually turn in the opposite way. Let's say that you're asking your spouse if they have a problem with you throwing a party this weekend. They might state "no problem" to keep the peace, but they could also end up nodding their heads up and down in a way that usually lets us know that the other person disagrees. This isn't necessarily manipulative, as they might just want to be nice and make the other person happy. It's still an example of how our heads can move oppositely of what we're trying to say, revealing our true intentions. What is their tension like? Do they have a clenched jaw? Look at the corner of their jaw right below their ear. You will be able to see if they are really holding their jaw clenched at this point, depending on their facial structure. We all clench our jaws from time to time, especially if we're experiencing constant stress.

However, rapid clenching and grinding can indicate that they are thinking deeply, which might mean that they are lying. If they're scratching their heads or picking at something, they might be a little confused. They could be searching for more understanding, but it could also indicate that they are looking for a better lie to cover their tracks.

How to Predict Others

Sometimes we just look at the pattern of behavior of people based on their actions alone. We think that this is the way that they are going to act in any given situation. People show a lot through their actions, but it's important to still pay special attention to the decisions others are making to see if there is a hidden truth. Make sure that you understand the full context of the way in which others are sharing their actions with others. You don't want to make assumptions just gathered from the basic understanding of a person. For example, you might have an acquaintance who is frequently hanging out in your circle of friends. This person is very closed off and quiet. They aren't very friendly to you, so you assume they don't like you. You have predicted that if you invited them out for a solo hangout session, they would decline.

However, you might not realize that this person is just very socially anxious.

They don't do well in group settings but would absolutely love to get to know you one-on-one. You only made an assumption based on the basic level of understanding of this person, but there was a hidden truth overlooked when connecting these dots. Don't let one single outlier be a reason that you assume someone is going to act in a certain way. Maybe you meet someone for the first time at a party, and they end up getting really drunk. You might assume that they are an alcoholic, especially since they were so willing to go over their limit after meeting new people.

Later on, you might discover that the night they met you, they had just gotten out of a relationship and wanted to let loose at the party after an especially hard day. Don't make assumptions based on what you have already learned. Consider other aspects to help you determine the entire truth or the bigger picture. Get to know other people. Study human behavior! Always question why others do the things that they do. Understand the motives behind others. What is it that they really want? Are they searching for a greater truth? Are they fulfilling an empty part of themselves? Are they trying to make connections? Are they simply bored? Decide if people are passive or if they are active.

Do they let others do as they please and remain calm and composed throughout the situation? Are they more likely to assume leadership positions with or without prompting? Are they reactionary or do they think more slowly? Will they give themselves a moment to think through their emotions and then respond, or will they jump and be aggressive at the first sign of a threat? The more you practice analyzing others and going over data collected in your head, the easier it becomes to be able to persuade them and protect yourself from other's control.

Chapter 6 : Dark Psychology Steps

Now that you have a basic level of understanding of how manipulation and persuasion work, it is crucial that you begin to understand the more intermediate methods that some might use on you in order to get you to fall for their biggest deceptions. These are never for you to use yourself. We are only sharing them with you so that you are able to really see the most embedded methods that other manipulators will use to keep you under their control. The more aware and prepared you are of these dark psychology steps, the easier it will be to stop this manipulation from controlling you and taking your life in any direction other than what you want. When you first start to crack open yours and others' mentality, it will be easier to pick up on little cues as you go along. Remember that it will always be a practice.

At first, you might think that you can make easy assumptions and that you have it all figured out. There will always be layers to all of the truths you are uncovering. You might have realized that someone was manipulating you but look deeper. Why were they doing so? How did this affect you? What can you do to recover? There are still some steps here that you can understand to better avoid being manipulated, and, if you choose to, use for your own purposes. That is not advised, but then again, we can't manipulate you into not being a manipulator. We can remind you that doing these things will never give you what you want. They might seem to at first, but you are filling a hole with all the wrong things.

Eventually, you are going to need more power and more control. You will be addicted to the ability to manipulate others, and the simple things won't get you "high" anymore. You'll have to keep looking further and further for more ways that you can gain power over other people, and this is only going to hurt you the most in the end. You should never take advantage of someone else, but in harmless settings, such as getting something small you want or maybe closing a business deal, you can use these tactics. Perhaps you want to ask your parents for some money, so you do the persuasion preparation method. Maybe you are trying to get others to buy your company's flood insurance, so you use the fear and relief method. As long as you aren't maliciously trying to take from others, you can be assured that your persuasion is positive.

Victimization

There are true victims in the world. Though we all have choices we can make, those that are abusive can take this ability away from their victims. They will replace their victims' own thoughts with thoughts of their own, making the abused feel trapped and helpless. To be a victim isn't a bad thing at all. Not everyone will be able to help themselves from falling into the web of lies and deceit that many abusers create to trap their victims. Then there are those who will play the part of the victim all because they are looking to get sympathy from you. This doesn't happen as often as people think, but it is a method that some will use in order to get the things that they want. It is a way to tap into the sympathy and compassion of those who are close to the manipulator in order to make them fall under their "spell." This is also a method of distraction.

If you tell someone that they hurt you, they can say, "Well, you hurt me." This might make you think that you did something wrong, which turns the focus to you trying to apologize to them! They will flip the situation around so that you are no longer concerned with the issue that you brought up in the first place but instead are focused solely on ensuring that the abuser is taken care of at that moment. It is a common tactic to keep the manipulator from having to confront the real issues that they need to work through. This method is especially useful for those manipulators who will see the good in other people. They will be able to see that desire to care for others and use that to their advantage.

You can tell if someone is actually a victim or if they are playing the part by how they respond to compassion or care that might be directed toward them. If they are a real victim, they will be appreciative and receptive to the care. They will use it as a way to help themselves feel better, and they will have a strong desire to work through their issues. Those who use victimization will take care of everything they can. They won't want to change and will instead do their best to make others feel as bad as possible about hurting them. This method isn't going to work out in the long-run. People eventually grow tired of those that constantly put themselves in the middle of the drama. They will start to easily see through the wall of victimization that has been created and understand the intrinsic manipulation that has existed.

Fear and Relief

Fear and relief is the method of making someone scared and then being the one to provide the solution. It is like pushing someone off a cliff and then being the one to reach your hand out and save them just before it is too late. The idea of the manipulation here is to help show that you are a vessel for comfort. The part of you that created the fear in the first place is often overlooked and not always realized initially.

This is common in long-term relationship abuse situations. Think of a parent who always terrifies the child about the outside world. They might tell scary stories of all that could happen if the child were to ever leave home. Perhaps they are giving the child wild ideas about the outside world. But the parent will still act as the savior, making sure that the child always stays close by. They will use bad situations to validate their reasoning as well. A child might feel trapped by their parents, one day deciding to sneak out at night. They might end up getting into trouble, and when that is revealed to the controlling parent, they might say something like, "See, I told you something bad would happen!" This is a tactic that is often used by advertisers as well. It is less harmful in this scenario and would be the method that you might use should you be selling something that would help to alleviate a person's fear.

For example, a plumbing company might share a scary fact about frozen pipes during the winter season, helping to sell more high-quality pipes and replacement services. You might not have initially been thinking about frozen pipes, but now you are, so you want to buy their service. It's not totally vindictive, as it could be a real problem that can be prevented. If you feel as though someone is trying to manipulate you with this method, make sure that you are first aware of the threat that they're trying to make you believe. Are they inflating the issue? Is it really something that you need to spend time being afraid of? Are you in the middle of manipulation, or are you actually enlightened now by this new, fearful information? The thing is that the abuser will never be the aggressor.

They want to show compassion. They won't be evil and scary in this situation because they are trying to show the abused that fear is an outside source. They desire to be the ultimate point of comfort, so they won't show their aggressive side, as that would then make them too scary to be dependable. If used in a gentle way, this method will not be so damaging. You should just focus on showing them the ways that you can help offer solutions for the true threat that already exists. Don't use fear alone to make them buy something. Use awareness to help enlighten them as to why it would be beneficial for them to invest in your product.

Sometimes, there is good news and bad news in a situation. It is important that you state the bad news first and then the good news. This can be your way of using the fear and relief method. Think of the way that a doctor would tell patients about certain health conditions and frame it in a way that will actually get the patient to do what they need to do in order to improve their health. For example, let's say that a patient is at risk for heart disease because they don't exercise and eat really unhealthily. The bad news is that they are a high-risk patient. The good news is that this can be reversed with a healthy diet and exercise. There are a few ways that this can be framed in order for the doctor to have a positive influence and actually get what he wants from this scenario. Here are the two alternative methods:

● "Unfortunately, we've discovered that you are a high risk for heart failure and other cardiovascular conditions. These kinds of conditions can be very risky and with your age and health status, they won't be so easily reversed. You can seriously reduce your risk and prevent these from happening if you start on the DASH diet and exercise at least three times a week."

● "It looks like you're going to have to start eating healthier and exercising. If you don't, you make your chances of having heart failure higher than they already are."

The first one is going to work out better for the patient and will likely have a higher chance of actually influencing them in the right direction. The first one lays out a fear. It paints a really serious situation that could scare the patient. However, then the solution is offered, and the patient's fear is reduced, making them more likely to continue with whatever will make them feel better. The second one kind of paints both as "bad news." It discusses first what the patient has to do and then follows with even more bad news. They are likely going to leave the appointment feeling bad about themselves and hopeless, whereas the first has a higher chance of inspiring positive influence into that patient.

Likability and Flirtation

If you want people to trust you, then it is important that you are likable. This is so much easier said than done! Many of us have been trying since before junior high to try and get people to like us. However, don't fear! Now that we are older and more emotionally aware, it's going to be a lot simpler to really see the ways that we can get others on our side. This is a harmless method for you to use! If you are truly charming, then others will be able to like you more. If you are a likable person, that will involve you being kind, funny, smart, and compassionate. None of these are bad, so of all the methods in the book, this is the best one for you to use with others.

The biggest thing you will have to be sure of is that you aren't losing yourself, or your happiness, in the process. If you are bad at being charming and people can see through your flirting, then only you will be the one suffering in the end. You might be able to charm some people, but there will still be the experts that can cut right through the façade. Start first by making sure that your emotional reactions are under control. If you are someone who reacts angrily to news or can't handle the slightest change in a schedule, then it might be a little more challenging for others to get along with you. Be very aware of the way that your face might appear to others. We're not talking about having an ugly or pretty face, of course. Keep your eyebrows relaxed with a slight smile.

If you show happiness and positivity on your face, more people will be likely to respond. Use open body language and engage with them in conversation. Don't just talk about yourself. Be giving and caring. Go out of your way to do things for them, no matter how small. Have an overall positive attitude and always look on the bright side. Don't force this positivity on others, of course. If someone is in a bad mood, don't tell them to "suck it up, things can be worse!" That's true, but that's not going to help them. Instead, say something like, "I'm sorry you're going through that.

Things will get better, and I'm here to help if you need me." Don't be afraid to show your passionate and enthusiastic side. Some individuals get scared of showing their vulnerability because that means they might look weak to others. Don't let this stop you from sharing the love that you have and that others deserve. Get creative with the compliments you give. Don't just pick up on oneliners from others that you hear. If you really want to be charming, it's time for you to get creative and come up with some substantial ways of impressing other people.

Persuasion Preparation

There are some ways for you to get prepared before you start to ask for whatever it is that you want. This will be like prepping them to say "yes" in order for things to work out in your favor. What you might want to do first is to offer them something. This is the reciprocity concept. If you give them something, they might be more likely to feel as though they should return the favor. If you invite them over to dinner, then they might be more likely to want to bring a bottle of wine or to take you out to dinner the next week. Another method is to ask for something small first. If you want to ask someone to do a chore for you, you might ask, "Do you mind sweeping?" Then after they agree, maybe you add in, "Could you take out the garbage, too, if you get a chance?" That makes it sound like two simple tasks rather than the long list of chores it could be when all grouped together. When making a deal, it might be a good idea to ask for something greater than what you are actually hoping for.

If you need to borrow $3,000 from a friend, you might ask first for $5,000. They will then propose a lower price because they don't have the full amount, but they are still going to give you what you initially needed because you primed the question by asking for more. Always look for how you can better persuade before you go into a meeting as opposed to after. Be prepared to get the things that you want, and you will start to discover it's so much easier to start to see the power come back into your own life, especially the power that was taken away from you initially by the manipulator.

Know Their Baseline

Get to really know the person and what they're all about before you try and persuade them. What are their interests? Are they a sports-oriented person? Would they rather go to an art museum in the afternoon? When you can understand some of the things that make them who they are, it can be easier to adapt to that personality, therefore, making it easier to persuade them later on. It is important to understand if someone has a thought that turns into a physical tick. If they're confused, do they scratch their heads, or do they squint their brows? If they're mad, do they shake their leg or do they pucker their lips? Start to associate what they are doing physically with what they are thinking so you can get more clarity about the way that they are acting. It is important to look for differences in the way that they might be acting to really get a sense of whether or not they're lying or trying to persuade you.

If they start to stray from some of the baselines that you already know them for, perhaps they are trying to change into a different person and become more influential. The methods that will help to persuade you will not work for everyone else. Just because you are easily influenced by certain aspects doesn't mean that others are going to be the same. Cater to personal strengths and weaknesses. The best method for salespeople is to make the buyer feel as though they are an individual. Get to know them on a personal level and they will be more likely to respond in a positive and healthy way. The companies that thrive the most are those that work off making you feel like you are the only person in the world. In order to really make someone feel like this, you have to know them and what their world is.

Chapter 7 : Dark Psychology Case Studies

What does all that we have discussed mean so far? Is there anything substantial to be taken from this information? This might be starting to all make sense in your own personal world, but perhaps you are wondering if there are other situations in the world that can help you to better understand what this all means in your world. It can be easy to feel isolated and have trouble relating to other people, but there are scientific situations that help us to better understand the complexities of our relationships and emotions. We have three different case studies here that will help you to better understand what it is that exists within us as people that might lead us to want to manipulate others. When we study other humans, we are looking at them in a controlled environment. This helps because oftentimes, the most that we know is based on our own personal experiences. It can lead us to wonder, "Is it just me, or is it everybody?" Case studies like these help us to understand the human condition rather than just ourselves as individuals.

The first study we will look at gives us a little insight into human behavior. In times when one leader can convince millions of people to believe the things that they do, it is important that we understand just how powerful some figures of authority can be. The better you can identify those who might attempt to manipulate you, the easier it will be to protect yourself in the long run.

The second study will help us understand exactly what we should be asking in order to determine if someone we know might be a narcissist. Since many manipulators are so good at covering their tracks and being deceptive, you never really know who might be trying to manipulate you. It is best if we start to ensure that we know how to identify a narcissist so that we never fall under their control.

The third study is one that will involve what manipulation in the future looks like. As we become more aware of what's going on around us, will it be harder to manipulate consumers? What might businesses do when those with purchasing power are no longer easily convinced? Rather than only thinking of manipulation as a tactic used between two individuals, we have to understand how a large group of people can be manipulated by a powerful institution.

The Milgram Experiment

How often have you found yourself doing something you don't want just because an authority figure told you that it was OK to do so? Maybe at work, a boss told you to do something against the rules, and you did just because you figured that no one else would get hurt in the process. They're the ones in charge, after all, so if they say it is OK, why wouldn't it be? We often don't realize just how powerful authority figures can be aside from the standard methods of control that we expect from them.

The Milgram experiment was an experiment led by psychologist Stanley Milgram in 1963 to determine the effects of social influence through authority figures. He set out to see how individuals might react when they are prompted to do something that might go against basic moral ideologies. The study started with several participants, called "teachers," who were under the impression that they were just to be assisting in an experiment, not the actual subject. The "teachers" were the ones in charge of administering electrical shocks to other "volunteers."

The teachers are the ones that were chosen for the study and were not given the information that they would be the ones that were actually studied. Part of the experiment meant keeping the teachers from knowing the true intention of the experiment. The "volunteers" were actors. The teachers were told that the point of the experiment was to see how the volunteers would react to physical punishment when they weren't able to properly learn something. The volunteers were highly aware of the actual study, and they were known as the "learners."

The teachers thought that the study was going to help see how the learners were able to better retain information when what they were taught was done so with physical stimuli. The learner was hooked up to a device that would administer a shock. The teacher was told to read different pairings of words to the learner, who would then repeat those pairs back to the teacher. The teacher would also be responsible for giving a shock to the learner when they got the answer wrong. The teacher thought that the point of the study was to see if this electrical shock when giving a wrong answer would help the learner to provide the right answer more frequently. The teacher and the learner could not see each other during this experiment.

Throughout the test, the voltage of each shock got continuously higher. In reality, the learner wasn't feeling any of the pain because there was no actual shock. Since they were out of sight, they were able to use prerecorded noises to indicate the levels of pain that they were experiencing in response to the pretend shock. They would play a tape recording of them in agony, but the teacher couldn't see, so they didn't know that this was all fake. They believed that each shock actually harmed the learner. Everyone was in on it, and no one was actually feeling any physical pain. The teacher was the only one who didn't know what was going on, and they were the person solely in charge of administering pain to other people.

If the teacher decided that they wanted to stop, then the instructor of the experiment, who knew everything that was going on, had to say one of a few selected phrases. These included things like, "please continue" or "you have no other choice, you must go on." These were the only phrases that the experiment conductor would say, and the teacher would have to decide whether they should listen to them or not. This is a pretty good setup for an experiment, so what ended up happening? Before even getting into that,

Milgram asked his students at Yale where he was teaching at the time what they thought. Most reported that they didn't believe that anyone would take this experiment too far. They assumed the teachers would stop when the pain became too much for the learner. They were wrong. What ended up happening in this instance is that the experiment conductor would tell the teacher to administer very painful shocks.

Each shock was more and more intense, to the point that it would have actually killed the learner had it been real. The point of the experiment was just to see how far the teachers would go when told to continue by an authority figure. Would they stop and stick to their morals, or would they blindly listen to the experiment leader and continue giving higher and more deadly electric shocks to the people on the receiving end? Would they cause others pain just because they were told to keep going? On average, at least 60% of participants or "teachers" wanted to stop before they reached the fatal shock but kept going, although this varied some based on area and demographic.

This means that on average, 6 out of 10 people blindly listened to the authority figures and administered shocks even though some of the dosages could have been fatal and they themselves wanted to quit. This was a very enlightening study just a few decades after so many innocent lives were taken during the Holocaust. Looking back on such horrifying acts of violence and the massive genocide that occurred, people may wonder, "How could so many people participate in this?" Experiments like this help show that it is much easier to influence others than many think, especially when they're completely unaware that they're being influenced (Milgram, 1963).

Are You a Narcissist?

There are many different ways that you can determine if someone is a narcissist. You can look at all of the things that we've discussed so far to see if they have any of the traits that we've mentioned. You can get to know them deeper and try to pick out any manipulative tactics that they have. You could give them a psychological test to determine whether or not they fit the description. But, there's one way that's easier than all of these to determine whether or not someone is actually a narcissist. Ask them outright: "Are you a narcissist?" It seems pretty simple and almost like a joke. However, studies have shown that this is one of the best questions to see if someone is a narcissist. There is a 40-question quiz that one can take in order to determine whether or not they are a narcissist.

That test proves to be more thorough; however, we're not all psychologists who will be able to administer personality tests like this. It is important that we identify these narcissists because they are going to be the ones who are the master manipulators we need to look out for. In order to protect yourself, you can ask this question when getting to know someone. In 11 different experiments administered to over 2,500 participants, they were all given a 40-question test to determine if they were a narcissist, and then they were also asked to answer the singular question we listed above.

The results were compared to see what people who were actually narcissists might say. During the test administered, there were some surprising findings to discover whether or not someone was a narcissist. Those who answered that they were a narcissist, or at least that they had narcissistic traits, were more likely to respond with pride in their behavior. Rather than being slightly ashamed to admit that they were a narcissist, considering narcissists' terrible reputation, they would boast about their abilities to prove that they are more narcissistic than others. The key here is that those who are narcissistic will not see themselves as having anything wrong with them. They believe that this is the way that life is supposed to be and that all of their behavior is justified. They will be happy to show that they might be more arrogant.

They will not try to hide the personality traits that they have as a narcissist. Instead, they will actually brag about their level of confidence and the way that they might be able to control others. Those who might still believe they are narcissists but really aren't going to be more likely to be ashamed of some of the egotistical tendencies that they might share. We all have certain traits or have done things in the past that outside of the context of our lives could be seen as narcissistic. We've all told a white lie, been jealous of other people, or put our needs first when we could have helped others. The difference between the average person and a narcissist is that we know these things are wrong. We know that it is better to choose the other option and that we might have certain things that we need to work on.

The average person might do something slightly narcissistic, but they will at least know afterward that they should have chosen to do something different. This isn't the most detailed way of figuring out who is a narcissist, but it is essential for the common people to understand how to identify a narcissist (Van Der Linden, 2016). Next time you are on a date or meeting new people, you might try to casually slip in the question. Maybe you talk about a narcissist from your past, or maybe you outright ask the question in a playful way.

If they state that they are and are proud, that's a red flag. If they state that they are and they're ashamed, or that they aren't, then this can be a good sign. You will be able to see how someone might really believe they are when you start asking simple questions like this. If you want to truly protect yourself from vicious manipulators, then this is the way to go. If you ever ask yourself, "Am I a narcissist?" and are fearful of the answers, that's a good sign that you aren't as narcissistic as you might believe.

Facebook's Unknown Manipulation Experiment

Facebook has hundreds of millions of users, so it is safe to say that this is one of the top sites that many people frequent. The number continues to grow and likely will for a long time. It is a powerful tool that shapes the way our society operates in some ways. Some of us upload personal information, while others simply share a few things here and there. We all have that one friend who posts and update every hour, and then there are the people on there who we forget we were friends with in the first place.

Regardless of what you are posting on Facebook, what matters most is how you interact with posts. Facebook makes billions of dollars from ad revenue alone, so the advertising world is an important market for them to tap into. Without ads, it is safe to say that Facebook wouldn't be as powerful as it is today. How does this app affect our emotional state? In one study, Facebook took almost 700,000 user's profiles and manipulated what was shown on their feed. They would show some happy things and some more damaging things that don't give off good feelings.

Then, at the end of the week, they focused on what the person who saw these images might share themselves. The results were basically what researchers expected when they set out to test these theories in the first place. The profiles that were exposed to sadder pictures throughout the week were more likely to have sad pictures at the end of the week. Those who were given happy images were more likely to have joyous posts. While we can assume this would be the case, it is still enlightening to see it actually happen. There was an uproar with this experiment because many people said it wasn't ethical (Meyer, 2014).

Facebook does have users agree to certain terms, one of them being that they're allowed to do what they want with user information. However, many ask if this is morally right since it involves the unknown manipulation of the user's emotions. Regardless of the ethics, the data still exists. You should ask yourself if you believe this is right or not to determine your own morals. Regardless of what conclusion you reach, this actual study still exists to remind us just how easily someone might be able to fall under the emotional control of a bigger corporation like Facebook.

This is just a reminder of how even minimal exposure can cause different emotional manipulation. Other advertisers can know whether or not they will be able to use your emotions based on the things that they show you first. We have to be highly aware of the subliminal messages that advertisers and other market experts are using on us in order to get the things that they want—our money.

Chapter 8 : Final Advice on Dark Psychology

Before finishing up the book, there are a few things that you should remember as you continue on this journey. It will take some time to get used to yourself. If you are recovering from manipulation, then it's likely that this is a process that's going to take some time. You will have to retrain your brain to get the voice of your abuser under control. You will also have to really get to know and understand people. You won't just want to focus on understanding yourself and the things that make up who you are. It's crucial that you pay attention to others and how they are acting as well. Let every experience you have of watching other humans give you a little insight into what makes a person decide to act in a certain way.

Look online at different documentaries that are available that could help to give you a little more insight into how and why someone might act a certain way. Even certain reality shows might be a way that you pick up on how other people are acting. The world is your library.

<u>What You Put Out Will Come Back</u>

It can be really easy to negatively manipulate someone, and doing positive persuasion might be a little harder. Negative manipulation just involves emotional reactions and blatant control. Positive persuasion is slower and takes time to master. However, this is also the method that is going to be more successful overall. Whatever energy you put out into the world will come back at you. It doesn't matter whether you believe in karma or not. If you manipulate everyone in your life, eventually, you will have no one left. It might work out for a while, but it is not substantial.

It is like using rotten wood to try and build a foundation. It is like trying to cover up an infected wound with makeup. It is like painting plastic gold. It is fake, and it will eventually fall through and end up not working out the way that you might have planned. Positive persuasion will turn you into an influencer. Once you start to gain a little bit of influence, you will find that it only becomes easier to increase this amount. You might be someone now who has gone through years of their own mental abuse. Don't let this pain be something that you give to someone else.

Work through it and let that be a driver for you to do better in the future, not an excuse to feel even more hurt. Maybe you were the abuser and you wanted to get to know a little more about why you might do the things that you do. Hopefully, you have gained some insight so you know how to best handle others and manipulation going forward. Always remember that what you do to other people will eventually come back to you.

Never Make Assumptions

Don't ever allow yourself to fall into a place where you think you know something. Once we start to make full assumptions, we are limiting our minds. Don't try to add up open-ended information and let that be a conclusion. You should only focus instead on the ways that you can investigate further. Just because someone has tried a manipulative tactic with you does not mean that they are an evil person who needs to be removed from your life. We will not always be aware of the way that we might be subconsciously manipulative. Assumptions are the easiest road that you can take. They are the shortcut, but that means that you are going to overlook a lot along the way. You will stop really digging deep into psychology when you only ever make assumptions about certain things. If you are not careful, you can fall into a place where you only think negatively. When you make assumptions, you are making guesses.

If you do this, you will miss a ton of valuable information along the way.

What to Do If You Get Caught in a Lie

Of course, you should never lie. However, if you do ever get caught in one, there are a few things that you can do to ensure that your reputation isn't ruined forever. It's always better to admit your mistakes and grow rather than pretending like you never lied in your life. There might be times when you say something exaggerated that gets misconstrued. The worst thing you could do right off the bat is to get defensive. Don't deny other people's feelings. Listen to them. The best possible thing that anyone could ever do is to just own up to the lie. Yes, it might be hard to admit that you are wrong, but everyone already knows the truth. Apologize for any wrongdoing that you might have done.

An apology should never be, "I'm sorry… but." That "but" is going to diminish your apology entirely. Explain yourself, but don't use it as an excuse. "I did this because" is better than "I only did this because." It's a minor difference, but it's still a way to show that you aren't trying to excuse whatever it is that you did that could have hurt others. Don't cover up the lie with another lie. You are just digging yourself into a deeper hole. That is the worst possible option that you could take if caught in a lie. It seems easier momentarily, but always consider what a bigger mess it might make down the line. The best way to avoid this is to just never lie in the first place!

Work on Yourself First

It will eventually become a natural process to look deep within yourself to find a greater understanding of who you, and humans in general, really are on the inside. In the beginning, make sure you are paying special attention to taking care of your own mental health. It is very easy to look at someone else and see their problems and know exactly what they need to do to fix their lives. This can sometimes just be a method of distracting ourselves from our own problems, so be cautious of doing this. Did you ever go over to someone else's house and see their junk lying around and think, "Wow, it is so easy to clean this; why is it like this?" But at the same time, you might have had your own personal mess in the corner.

That's because it's easy to see other's problems since we are removed from them. If you pay too much attention to fixing other people, then you will start to forget about yourself in the process. It is also important to look at your own problems because they might be the very things that you are recognizing in others that need to be fixed. A lot of the hard lessons we have to learn in life we do so on our own. You can't control other people! You can only persuade them. Always remember to look for ways to improve overall.

<u>Remember Your Rights</u>

One of the most important steps in overcoming emotional manipulation and abuse is to remember your rights. Remember all the things that you are owed and that you deserve in this life. Once you start to forget this, it becomes easier for others to come into your life and take advantage of you. You have the right to say "no" whenever you please. Sometimes, it's scary. You might be that kind of passive person who is more concerned with pleasing other people than you are with taking care of your own needs. Remember that anyone who truly cares about you is going to accept the times when you choose to say "no."

You might be afraid that they will leave you or that they won't want to be your friend anymore, but if this is the case, then good riddance! You don't need that kind of toxic energy in your life, so it's best that you separate yourself from this kind of person sooner rather than later. If you don't allow yourself the ability to stand up for your rights, others are going to take advantage of this. You deserve the right to feel however you want. It is the reaction that might not always be acceptable.

For example, you have the right to be angry that your sports team lost. You do not have the right to throw the TV across the room because of this if this is a public space for the family. If you live alone and you paid for the TV, by all means, throw it, but remember that the reaction is separate from the emotion. No one is allowed to tell you that you don't feel a certain way. You know your emotions, and you are allowed to own up to them. You have the right to enjoy the things that you like.

Even if it's the worst movie ever made, a terrible song that is overplayed on the radio, or an actor everyone else hates, you like what you like! Anyone who shames you, belittles you, and makes you feel bad about these choices is not someone that you should be concerned about impressing! You deserve the right to make your own decisions. This is the same as having the right to say "no," but remember, as long as you're not hurting anyone else, it is your body, your mind, your life, and your choice. If you want to go to a college out of state, do it. If you want to be a marine biologist, do it. If you want to binge-watch a TV show on your weekend off, do it. Don't let anyone else control your actions! You have the right to do whatever makes you happy and brings you closer to the life that you deserve!

It's OK to Walk Away

Often, the people who use the darkest psychology on us are the people that we are closest to. They might be your mother, father, sister, husband, neighbor, boss, girlfriend, and so on. No matter who it is, remember that you do not owe anyone a single thing. If they are emotionally abusing you, get out of there as fast as you can. It can be hard to just up and walk away. Not everyone is going to have the emotional ability to just leave as they please. You might live with your parents or have children with your spouse. Maybe your boss abuses you but you can't leave because they might tarnish your name.

Remember that most of the time, the negative side effects of leaving the abuser are never going to be as bad as experiencing the pain they inflict over and over again. You might struggle to separate yourself, but it is this manipulator that put the idea in your head that you are not allowed to leave or that you won't be able to survive without them. Sometimes you might be able to work out a relationship, but it is not your duty to fix them. You have to focus on yourself first. Always remember the airplane scenario involving oxygen masks.

The flight attendant will tell you to put yours on first before you help anyone else because, by the time you are done helping others, you will have died yourself! Your needs should be your top priority, and from there, you might be able to work through other's issues in order to build a stronger, healthier relationship.

www.ingramcontent.com/pod-product-compliance
Lightning Source LLC
LaVergne TN
LVHW011304210726
843509LV00016B/789